CONTEMPORARY
POLITICAL IDEOLOGIES
A comparative analysis

N

THE DORSEY SERIES IN POLITICAL SCIENCE

CONTEMPORARY POLITICAL IDEOLOGIES

A comparative analysis

LYMAN TOWER SARGENT
University of Missouri—St. Louis

1972 • Revised Edition

THE DORSEY PRESS, Homewood, Illinois 60430
IRWIN-DORSEY LIMITED, Georgetown, Ontario

Revised Edition

First Printing, March, 1972

Library of Congress Catalog Card No. 72–176054

Printed in the United States of America

To
Evan

WHO DIDN'T HELP ME
ON THIS EDITION
SO IT GOT FINISHED ON TIME

PREFACE

The world today is influenced by many different views of life. Everyone has heard the names of most of them, but when we hear the words communism, democracy, nationalism, and so forth, we react to them emotionally. We immediately view one as good, another as bad. We seldom, if ever, make the effort to understand what these words in fact mean. This reaction is due to our acceptance, whether consciously recognized or not, of one or more of these views of life. Most people today are sadly lacking in knowledge of these ideologies. We do a disservice to modern students when we fail to introduce them to the wide range of belief systems that exist in the world today. It is the purpose of this book to present the essential features of some of these belief systems objectively and understandably. It is my basic assumption that an accurate, unbaised presentation of the ideas that underlie these ideologies must be the primary concern of any such book. If the author allows his own bias—and he will have one—to color the presentation of the material, he is doing a great disservice to his readers and to the ideology he accepts. Therefore, I have attempted to avoid any encroachment of my personal opinion into the body of this work.

The revised edition has been largely rewritten, and I have attempted to reorganize where needed and to tighten the argument wherever possible. Different people will wish to emphasize different ideologies and will want to use this book as an overview of all the important ideologies. At the end of each chapter the reader who is interested in more extensive analyses of the ideology will find a list of additional readings that include a variety of more or less objective studies and some of the advocates and opponents of the ideology. I have tried to list the most important books plus a wide enough variety to represent most of the points of view involved. Where this is impossible, I have tried to list some bibliographies. Most of the books listed are available in paperback. Since the availability of paperback books changes rapidly, I have not tried to indicate which ones are in paperback. The student who wants to find out should consult *Paperbound Books in Print,* which can be found in any library and most bookstores.

If we are to understand these ideologies, we cannot treat them in complete isolation from one another—we must carefully compare them. This I have done throughout the book. In the concluding chapter I have brought this material together in a systematic manner and added to it to produce, by way of summary, a short comparative analysis of the ideologies.

Again, as with any book, this one has benefited by the efforts of others. My greatest debt is to those who adopted the first edition for their courses, for, without their support, this edition would have truly been impossible. Due to space limitations I cannot thank all those who have helped me in my preparation of this edition. My greatest thanks go to Mrs. Peggy Braden who typed the original manuscript and who kept the duties of department chairman light enough so that I could find the time to write. Thomas Zant read the first edition very carefully and provided me with his comments and the comments of his students. Many others made briefer comments. Since I did not take all the advice given me, they are not to be held responsible for the result.

Again this book is dedicated to my son, whose help on the first edition so impeded its progress. He did not help on this edition, and I finished it ahead of schedule.

February, 1972   LYMAN TOWER SARGENT

CONTENTS

1
INTRODUCTION

There is much controversy today among political scientists, sociologists, and others about the meaning and affect of ideology. I shall avoid this debate as much as possible because it seldom relates to the purpose of this book—the presentation of the major political ideologies in the world today.[1]

The whole approach of the book assumes that ideologies do affect people and in this chapter I shall suggest a number of ways in which this might take place. But these assumptions can be taken simply as assumptions that hopefully we will learn more about in time. So far the effects of ideologies have not been tested carefully enough to allow for certainty, but my assumption that they do affect people is widely accepted as a reasonable one.

First let us look at the general concept of ideology.

An ideology is a value or belief system that is accepted as fact or truth by some group. It is composed of sets of attitudes toward the various institutions and processes of society. It provides the believer with a picture of the world both as it is and as it should be, and, in so doing, it organizes the tremendous complexity of the world into something fairly simple and understandable. The degree of organization and the simplicity of the resulting picture vary considerably from ideology to ideology, and the ever-increasing complexity of the world tends to blur all the pictures. At the

---

[1] The reader who is interested in the current controversy over the nature of ideology should consult the suggested readings at the end of the chapter.

1

same time, the basic pictures provided by the ideologies seem to remain fairly constant.

But a distinction should be made between a simple belief in something and an ideology. An ideology or a belief system can be clearly distinguished from an individual's belief in something. An ideology must be a more or less interrelated collection of beliefs that provide the believer with a fairly thorough picture of the entire world.

There have been a number of useful definitions of ideology proposed which may help us understand the word. Samuel P. Huntington defines ideology as ". . . a system of ideas concerned with the distribution of political and social values and acquiesced in by a significant social group."[2] Robert E. Lane defines political ideology as follows:

I shall use the term "political ideology" to mean a body of concepts with these characteristics:

1. They deal with the questions: Who will be the rulers? How will the rulers be selected? By what principles will they govern?
2. They constitute *an argument*; that is, they are intended to persuade and to counter opposing views.
3. They integrally affect some of the major values of life.
4. They embrace a program for the defense or reform or abolition of important social institutions.
5. They are, in part, rationalizations of group interests—but not necessarily the interests of all groups espousing them.
6. They are normative, ethical, moral in tone and content.
7. They are (inevitably) torn from their context in a broader belief system, and share the structural and stylistic properties of that system.[3]

Except for item one, which is overlimiting, Lane's definition of ideology is more carefully drawn than any other found in the literature on ideology. As can be seen in point one of his definition, Lane is concerned solely with *political* ideology narrowly defined. In this book we are concerned with political ideology in the context of Lane's first point, but we will also look at the relationship between political and social institutions. In effect, we will be discussing social and political ideology. We will deal only with ideologies that have a major and broad social and political

---

[2] Samuel P. Huntington, "Conservatism as an Ideology," *American Political Science Review*, vol. LI (June, 1957), p. 454.

[3] Robert E. Lane, *Political Ideology: Why the American Common Man Believes What He Does* (New York: Free Press of Glencoe, 1962), pp. 14–15. Emphasis in the original.

element and are predominately secular in nature. Adding philosophical, religious, and other beliefs that might be labeled ideological is beyond the scope of this book.

Prior to its current definition as outlined above, two major thinkers were noted for their use of the term *ideology,* Karl Marx and Karl Mannheim. Marx described as ideological any set of political *illusions* that have been produced by the social experiences of a class.[4] For Marx a person's membership in a particular class produces a picture of the world that is warped by the prejudices of the class. Thus, it would be virtually impossible for an individual class member to achieve an accurate concept of the world.

Karl Mannheim discussed the definition of ideology at great length without fundamentally changing Marx's conception of the term. He distinguishes two separate meanings of the word—the particular and the total. "The particular conception . . . is implied when the term denotes that we are skeptical of the ideas and representations advanced by our opponents. They are regarded as more or less conscious disguises of the real nature of a situation, a true recognition of which would not be in accord with his interests."[5] The total conception of ideology refers to ". . . the ideology of an age or of a concrete historical-social group, e.g. of a class, when we are concerned with the characteristics and composition of the total structure of the mind of the epic or of this group."[6] The particular conception contains the same elements as Marx's definition. The total conception, without the negative connotations of the particular conception, says the same thing about the individual's picture of the world as does Marx.

Definitions of ideology have changed somewhat from Marx's or even Mannheim's day to our own. They usually no longer contain the negative elements found in the previous definitions, but they all refer to the development of a world view by some group.

---

[4] It is interesting to note that contemporary Marxists do not consistently use the term in the same sense. See, for example, Clemens Dutt, ed., *Fundamentals of Marxism-Leninism. Manual,* 2nd rev. ed. (Moscow: Foreign Languages Publishing House, 1963), pp. 165–68.

[5] Karl Mannheim, *Ideology and Utopia: An Introduction to the Sociology of Knowledge,* trans. Louis Wirth and Edward Shils (New York: Harcourt, Brace, Jovanovich, Inc., 1936), p. 55.

[6] Ibid., p. 56.

An oversimplified and extreme example will help both to illustrate the nature of ideology and to explain the complex process of change within it. In the past, movies presented viewers with a simple, clearly defined view of the clash of the forces of good and evil in the American West. The good guys and the bad guys were even clearly identified by white clothes and a white horse for the hero and black clothes and a black horse for the villain. The good guys always won, and the hero rode off into the sunset without any entangling alliances to keep him from his next battle with evil.

Although much of the basic pattern is not changed and the identical pattern can be found in the type of science fiction known as "space opera," many "adult" Westerns today show the two sides dressed the same and riding the same color horses. In addition, some go so far as to present the bad guy as not really bad, simply misunderstood; and the good guy is not always the epitome of all virtue. Finally, the modern hero is often attracted to women, something that never would have occurred to the old white-hatted hero.

These differences illustrate some of the problems in analyzing ideologies as they change over time. We shall see in some belief systems or ideologies exactly the old, rigid good-bad division. In others we shall see such a complexity of factors at work that it will be difficult or even impossible to tell precisely the good guys from the bad guys. In these more complex ideologies, it is often found that the individual believer accepts more than one ideology. He accepts, for example, the positions of a political party, a church, and a business firm or labor union. Each of these positions constitutes either a partially or fully developed belief system or ideology, and, although certain aspects of these systems may coincide perfectly or closely enough to not cause conflict within the individual, other aspects may be widely divergent and may, if noticed, immobilize the individual because of the fundamental difference between the two beliefs held at the same time.

It should not be concluded that we all have ideologies. We all have beliefs, in large part gained from identification with or membership in some group, but, unless the beliefs are recognized or acted upon with or without recognition, it is difficult to say that we have an ideology. The various beliefs we hold may also not "constitute *an argument*" in Lane's phrase because they are sufficiently in conflict with each other to make either recognition or action impossible.

This conflict is most common in what we call a pluralistic society. In such a society there is no single official ideology. At the same time, it must be recognized that there are conflicting ideologies present in all societies. Assuming for the present that people select among ideological options, we can, by overstating the case, illustrate the dilemma presented by the pluralistic society. At the same time we must recognize that individuals do not generally choose an ideology but are brought up in such a way that they grow into their belief pattern without ever making a conscious choice. The individual in such a society is free to pick and choose among the variety of positions that are available to him. Many individuals will not be aware of the wide variety of ideologies that exist, but, when they are, they may become confused, apathetic, or inactive. On the other hand, the wide variety of ideological options available within an open system tends to de-emphasize ideology; the conflict within the individual, there-fore, does not become as important as it would within a system in which there were only a single official ideology and the individual found himself in conflict with that ideology.

Thus, we have the phenomenon that we noticed with the American movies of the old West. As society grows more and more complex, it be-comes harder and harder to present a simple division between good and bad, between the white and black hats. The black and the white are mixed and become grey. We have discovered that the world is not as sim-ple as the older movies would have us believe, and the new "adult" West-ern is a reflection of this recognition.

Even with this change in the pattern of some ideologies, they all at-tempt to organize our complex world into a pattern that will at least give some signposts to help the believer distinguish good from bad. And, finally, in all of them we shall see that the ideal and the reality do not quite meet, and we shall witness a struggle to get them to meet through changes either in the ideal or in the reality.

In addition, within any given society, different segments of the popula-tion will hold different ideologies. For example, within the United States today, probably the overwhelming majority, if asked, would label them-selves as believers in democracy. But some would call themselves an-archists, Fascists, and so forth, although it might well be true that many of them would not know what these terms meant. Every society exhibits a variety of ideologies. In no case will a given society be so completely dominated by a single ideology as to have no ideological alternatives available within the system.

As was noted above, many of those who are willing to label themselves democrats and so forth do not know the meaning of the terms they use or do not act in the way the ideology would be expected to lead them. Most people build up a pattern of behavior, some aspect of which comes directly from the dominant political ideology of the country in which they live. For example, if one thinks about it, it is surprising that people accept the outcome of elections rather than fighting for their side when they lose. But people are so conditioned to accept loss in elections that they do so without ever thinking about revolt. Although most behavior is probably not a result of the acceptance of an ideology, some seems to be.

Furthermore, there are differences within each major ideology that in effect make each one a cluster of ideologies. Democracy as an ideology is perhaps the most obvious example, being composed of two major categories—democratic capitalism and democratic socialism. All who place themselves in either of these categories would believe themselves to be democrats, and some of them see themselves as the only true democrats. In addition to this major division, there are numerous disagreements over the emphasis to be placed on certain aspects of democracy and over the tactics to be used in achieving the desired goals. This phenomenon is not characteristic of the democratic ideology alone but actually of all ideologies. As we know from reading the news from Eastern Europe in recent years, there are significant disagreements among Communists over what is essential to communism as an ideology and what is nonessential and can be changed, modified slightly, or completely discarded.

There is no ideology that is completely free from this sort of disagreement. When speaking of a single, official ideology, it should be recognized that even these so-called single, official ideologies are not completely monolithic but are composed of a variety of factions and disagreements that go together to make up the ideology and to allow it to change to meet changing conditions.

To reiterate, an individual may hold within himself a variety of beliefs that may be in conflict. Normally, of course, he does not recognize the conflicting or irreconcilable nature of these beliefs, but he applies them to different situations without ever viewing his values as a whole. An interesting example of this tendency can be found in the recent history of civil rights in the United States. Christianity is usually believed to teach that all men should be treated equally. The segregationist who professes Christianity has historically not been consciously aware of any disparity between his political and religious beliefs. As many churches have come to say that segregation does not fit with Christianity, the segregationist has normally responded in one of three ways. He may argue that the church should not involve itself in social or political affairs, or he may find justification within the Bible for his position, or he may gradually reject one of the two positions that appear to be in conflict.

Another example might be the man who thoroughly believes that the majority should rule, and just as thoroughly believes that for a wide variety of reasons, such as the need for secrecy in foreign affairs, that the majority cannot and should not in fact be allowed to rule. Again, he will either fail to see the contradiction; or he will argue that they are not irreconcilable by saying, for example, that the people actually rule, even in foreign affairs, by checking the actions of their representatives at periodic elections; or he will gradually reject one of his two positions. This problem presents one of the most serious obstacles to a clear presentation and understanding of ideology, and it will of necessity remain a constant theme in the consideration of each ideology.

The seven ideologies that have been selected for consideration have been chosen on the basis of two main criteria: their importance in the world today and the desire to present the broad range of political beliefs. Nationalism, communism, and democracy clearly fall in the first category. Each one must be understood before one can intelligently grasp the news of the day. Anarchism clearly belongs in the second category. Never dominant for long in any area, it still has many adherents, is clearly growing considerably in popularity, and a survey of political ideology would not be complete if it ignored anarchism. Fascism and national socialism, the ideologies of the developing nations, and the New Left fall somewhere between these two categories. Each is important for an understanding of recent and contemporary history but not to the same degree as nationalism, communism, and democracy. In addition, each represents a point on the spectrum of political belief that is not clearly occupied by any of the others, although the New Left and anarchism are quite similar.

One of them, nationalism, is of a different type from all the others because it affects all the others. But nationalism is important just because it is commonly part of the other ideologies; therefore, it will be discussed first so that it will be possible to see the ways in which it affects the other ideologies. The others will follow in the order of the categories discussed above.

The wide variety of different types of ideologies raises a further difficult problem for the analyst. Since each ideology is significantly different from the others, there is no single approach appropriate to all of them. The problem is that each ideology emphasizes different aspects of society and may ignore other aspects that are stressed by another ideology. Therefore, it is not possible to treat each ideology in exactly the same way. It is necessary to present the ideology as it actually is rather than as we might think an ideology should be. Thus, each one will be analyzed as its own nature dictates.

At the same time it is necessary to compare them, and, in order to do so, some way must be devised so that a similar type of information is made available for each ideology wherever possible. This will not be entirely possible because of the different emphases found in each ideology.

In order to achieve some sort of comparability, the complex of interactions among individuals, groups, and institutions that we call society has been divided into five segments:

1. The value system
2. The socialization system
3. Social stratification and social mobility
4. The economic system
5. The political system

This breakdown is simply a very loose set of categories designed to provide some minimal order to the analysis of ideologies. As is indicated in the following paragraphs, these categories merely allow us to describe the attitudes found in the various ideologies; they do not provide any tool for analyzing the ideologies beyond mere description.

In its simplest formulation, an ideology consists of attitudes toward the various aspects of society. For example, the democratic ideology includes the notion that all citizens should be politically equal. Of course, even the most superficial analysis of the political system in the United States, a country that accepts the democratic ideology, shows that not all citizens are politically equal. This example illustrates a number of problems that one has when discussing ideology. First, it illustrates that ideologies are not necessarily put into effect by the society. Second, a glance at the civil rights movement and the Supreme Court decisions on reapportionment may show an influence of the ideology on the social system. Third, since not all people in the United States accept this notion of political equality, it demonstrates that, within modern, complex, pluralistic societies, there are a number of significantly different competing value systems that must be considered.

Any analysis of any part of society, including the value system, is an attempt to answer a series of questions regarding the various institutions and processes mentioned above. This series of questions can be divided into two parts. One asks how the society should function; the other asks how it does in fact function. The answers to the first part give one a picture of the value system. The answers to the second part give one a picture of the social system in operation.

From the point of view of the study of ideology, the value system of a society is its most important characteristic. In some ways, the value system *is* the ideology. But it should be kept in mind that unless one speaks of value systems rather than a value system, one is likely to radically oversimplify one's analysis. There is seldom one completely dominant value system or ideology within any given society. It is most appropriate, therefore, to speak of the value system as being made up of subsystems. In order to understand these ideologies, and particularly their value systems, we must comprehend the theoretical or philosophical basis of them. Much of each of the analyses of the ideologies will, therefore, be necessarily given over to a commentary on questions generally regarded as part of political philosophy.[7] In addition, each chapter will attempt to give some idea of the attitudes toward the various institutions and processes of society found in each ideology. It will be possible to see what questions are important to each ideology, and thus some basis will be established for comparing them.

Before this can be done, it will be necessary to understand a bit more about each of these institutions and processes. The socialization system is probably the most important and least understood segment of society. Socialization is the process by which each individual gains the values of the

---

[7] Loosely, political philosophy aims at an understanding of political values and norms. Political ideology is a value or belief system that is accepted as being correct.

society as his own. It is generally assumed that the most important institutions that effect the ways in which, and the degree to which, the individual gains these values are (1) the family system, (2) the educational system, (3) the religious system, and (4) a variety of other influences such as the mass media, the peer group, and so forth. We are not always sure of the mechanism by which the various institutions of socialization operate. It is, of course, fairly obvious that a child is strongly influenced in his whole outlook on life by his family environment and at least by his early school years. It is perhaps less clear how the other institutions of socialization influence an individual's outlook on life. We can perhaps assume that the same messages repeated over and over again in institutions that the individual has been taught to respect, such as the religious and educational systems, may have a cumulative effect and thus ultimately become part of the individual's value system. The mass media probably operates in the same way.

The social stratification system is the way in which the society ranks individuals within it. This ranking may be a very clearly defined class system or it may be very loose, with the lines between classes or status groups somewhat hazy. Social stratification is usually summed up within a political ideology by the question of equality. Some ideologies contain the notion that ideally there should be no social stratification at all. In other words, some people believe that everyone within the society should be equal in specified ways. For example, some talk about equality of opportunity and political equality; others believe in economic and social equality. Each of these points is important for an understanding of social stratification because only if there were no economic, social, political, or any other inequalities would there be no social stratification system. Almost no one has ever suggested such complete equality, but each of these more limited types of equality has been suggested or tried at various times and will be discussed later.

One of these types of equality, equality of opportunity, is particularly important in any society. Equality of opportunity means that no artificial obstacles or barriers should keep any individual or group from moving from one class to another if they have the ability. In essence, equality of opportunity defines certain parts of the social mobility system within a society. Every society has such a mobility system which determines the ease or difficulty with which an individual can move among classes or statuses in the society. The system also determines the basis for such movement. For example, in traditional China an individual could move into the upper classes of the society by successfully completing a series of examinations. Many contemporary societies have no such formal system but base mobility on such standards as wealth.

The economic system is concerned with the production, distribution, and consumption of wealth. The major parts of the economic system that will concern us relate to (1) production, (2) distribution and consumption, and (3) the relationship of the economic system to the political system. We shall be particularly concerned with questions concerning the degree of economic equality desired by the ideology and the means that the ideology sets for achieving this goal. Since most ideologies reject extremes of wealth and poverty that are too great, they have developed means of correcting the imbalance such as, for example, the graduated income tax or the nationalization of industries.

Most of the economic questions that we will discuss deal with more purely political questions. The political system is that segment of society that draws together or integrates all the others. The political system can make decisions that are binding upon the whole society, and thus it holds the key to any understanding of the whole ideological and social system. To some degree, a political ideology includes all of the above questions in one form or another.

Suggested readings

A good bibliography on the question of ideology can be found on pp. 369–73 of the volume edited by Richard H. Cox listed below.

Aiken, Henry D. *The Age of Ideology: The Nineteenth Century Philosophers.* Vol. V of *The Great Ages of Western Philosophy.* New York: George Braziller, 1958.

Apter, David E. (ed.). *Ideology and Discontent.* New York: Free Press of Glencoe, 1964.

Bergmann, Gustave. "Ideology." *Ethics,* Vol. LXI (April, 1951), pp. 205–18.

Christenson, Reo. M. et al. *Ideologies and Modern Politics.* New York: Dodd, Mead & Co., 1971.

Connolly, William E. *Political Science & Ideology.* New York: Atherton Press, 1967.

Cox, Richard H. (ed.). *Ideology, Politics, and Political Theory.* Belmont, Calif.: Wadsworth Publishing Co., 1969.

Dolbeare, Kenneth M., and Dolbeare, Patricia. *American Ideologies: The Competing Beliefs of the 1970's.* Chicago: Markham Publishing Co., 1971.

Germino, Dante. *Beyond Ideology: The Revival of Political Theory,* Parts I and II. New York: Harper & Row, 1967.

Gyorgy, Andrew, and Blackwood, George D. *Ideologies in World Affairs.* Waltham, Mass.: Blaisdell Publishing Co., 1967.

Huntington, Samuel P. "Conservatism as an Ideology." *American Political Science Review,* Vol. LI (June, 1957), pp. 454–73.

Kohn, Hans. *Political Ideologies of the 20th Century.* 3d ed. rev. New York: Harper & Row, 1966.

Lane, Robert E. *Political Ideology: Why the American Common Man Believes What He Does.* New York: Free Press of Glencoe, 1962.

Lichtheim, George. *The Concept of Ideology and Other Essays.* New York: Random House, 1967.

McClosky, Herbert. "Consensus and Ideology in American Politics." *The American Political Science Review,* 58 (June, 1964), pp. 366–82.

Mannheim, Karl. *Ideology and Utopia: An Introduction to the Sociology of Knowledge.* Trans. Louis Wirth and Edward Shils. New York: Harcourt, Brace, Jovanovich, Inc., 1936.

Preston, Nathaniel Stone. *Politics, Economics, and Power; Ideology and Practice Under Capitalism, Socialism, and Fascism.* New York: Macmillan Co., 1967.

Rejai, M.; Wilson, W. L.; and Beller, D. C. "Political Ideology: Empirical Relevance of the Hypothesis of Decline." *Ethics,* Vol. LXXVIII (July, 1968), pp. 303–12.

Shklar, Judith N. (ed.). *Political Theory and Ideology.* New York: Macmillan Co., 1966.

2
NATIONALISM

We hear the word *nationalism* quite often these days, usually in connection with a war or revolution. In North American newspapers, it is most commonly used with reference to the countries of Africa, Asia, or the Middle East. We also hear it used in relationship to the Latin American countries that are attempting to establish an image of their own, separate from that of the United States. Today we frequently hear the term in connection with minority movements within countries, such as the Black Nationalists in the United States, the Basques in Spain, and the French-Canadian Separatists in Canada. We seldom, if ever, think of ourselves as nationalists. If we think of ourselves in these terms at all, we view ourselves as patriotic. But, interestingly enough, the words *nationalism* or *patriotism* are rarely precisely defined. We react to these words emotionally. Nationalism is generally thought of as something bad. Patriotism is thought of as something good. The good American may be called patriotic, but not nationalistic. It takes only a modicum of reflection to recognize that they represent similar, perhaps even the same, phenomenon.

These judgments affecting the common usage of the terms makes their analysis doubly difficult. First, whatever one says is likely to fly in the face of common usage. Second, common usage seems to creep into analyses that are otherwise objective. However we define these terms, we must attempt to use them consistently in that manner and to avoid the emotional overtones that are so commonly associated with them. We must attempt to understand patriotism and nationalism as a view of the world, as a political ideology. And, since it is a political ideology that affects all other political ideologies, it must be viewed as a set of values that are accepted by many people whether they are labeled Communists or democrats or even anarchists.

It may also be valuable to view as a part of this set of phenomena the rejection of nationalism and patriotism through the acceptance of what we might label *internationalism*. Although there are probably very few people who view the whole world in the same way, with the same love that they view their own country, there are some who do. On the face of it, internationalism may seem to be a very different kind of phenomenon from nationalism. Without overdoing the analogy, perhaps we could compare the difference to the differing, but strong, feelings a man may have toward, for example, the state of Florida and the United States. Most people do have some sense of loyalty toward both their home state and the United States. Most people do not have a sense of loyalty to the world as a whole, but this is not to say that the feelings of those who do are essentially different from a man who feels strongly about both Florida and the United States. Internationalism is the same type of phenomena as patriotism and nationalism, and, perhaps by looking at all three, we shall be able to understand each one more thoroughly.

The problem of definition is the key problem here. We must be able to come up with definitions of nationalism, patriotism, and internationalism that will allow us to treat them objectively and will avoid the major emotional overtones that so often confuse the issue. Nationalism was first brought to the attention of most people either by World War I and the question of national self-determination or by the rise of fascism and national socialism and by World War II. It has been kept in the news by the breakup of colonialism in Asia and Africa, enhanced by the troubles in Vietnam and the Middle East. Nationalism therefore is equated with trouble and probably could not have been kept free from its negative connotations. Patriotism, at least in the United States, has a somewhat more positive tone to it. But patriotism today also refers to the 100-percent American, the one who is so patriotic that he cannot see anything good anywhere else in the world. Thus, patriotism can perhaps mean an unrealistic isolation and devotion to country. Internationalism is the most neutral of the three terms because there are so few examples of internationalists that the word has few emotional overtones. Strong emotions are

felt, however, by the 100-percent American who rejects the international-
ist position because he believes that it will lead to the destruction of his
country.

Theories of nationalism

A search of the literature on nationalism, and it is growing rapidly,
indicates that the major writers do not agree on what it is they are talking
about. For example, in his excellent study, *Nationalism and Social Communication,* Karl W. Deutsch points out that we do not know enough
about nationalism to be entirely sure what it is.[1] Boyd C. Shafer lists ten
beliefs that seem to him to be commonly present in the feeling of nationalism but goes on to say that "No claim is laid for their infallibility or
finality."[2]

Hans Kohn, perhaps the best known scholar on nationalism, defines it
as ". . . a state of mind, permeating the large majority of a people and claim-
ing to permeate all its members; it recognizes the nation-state as the ideal
form of political organization and the nationality as the source of all crea-
tive cultural energy and of economic well-being. The supreme loyalty of
man is therefore due to his nationality, as his own life is supposedly rooted
in and made possible by its welfare."[3] Unfortunately, Kohn constantly
impresses the reader that he is analyzing a system of belief that he thoroughly believes to be bad, and, although he strives for objectivity, he never
quite succeeds.[4] Another author who seems to have the same problem
says that nationalism ". . . holds that humanity is naturally divided into
nations, that nations are known by certain characteristics which can be
ascertained, and that the only legitimate type of government is national
self-government."[5]

As a first step in the direction of understanding nationalism, it should
be noted that there are a number of other terms that are similar to national-

---

[1] Karl W. Deutsch, *Nationalism and Social Communication: An Inquiry into
the Foundations of Nationality,* 2d ed. (Cambridge, Mass.: M.I.T. Press, 1966),
pp. 187–89.

[2] Boyd C. Shafer, *Nationalism, Myth and Reality* (New York: Harcourt, Brace,
Jovanovich, 1955), p. 7.

[3] Hans Kohn, *The Idea of Nationalism, A Study of Its Origins and Background*
(New York: Collier Books, 1944), p. 16.

[4] For example, see ibid., p. 13.

[5] Elie Kedourie, *Nationalism,* rev. ed. (London: Hutchinson University Library,
1961), p. 9.

ism in that all of them are concerned with a variety of ties or connections among individuals that somehow form a new entity, for example, such words and phrases as *community* and *public* or *national interest*. We can see this process in operation in a small, intimate collection of individuals, such as the family, which is made up of a group of individuals with different interests and, to some extent, different outlooks on life, but with something in common that helps them to form a unit. The family continues over generations and has an emotional unity which provides a basis for identification. But there is a considerable difference between the ties of a family and something as distant or abstract as a nation or the public. Nevertheless, there is at least one fundamental similarity: the recognition of both the family and the nation as an entity presupposes some sort of group consciousness.

Part of the problem here is found in the English language. It makes it difficult for us to speak of group identity without using hybrid terms. For example, when we speak of national interest, we probably want to imply that the nation is something separate from, and perhaps more than, the sum of the individuals that compose it. We can say that we are conscious of, or recognize, the nation or the public (a much more abstract entity), but the words do not have the emotional content that makes it possible to readily express a feeling of unity or identity.

An additional problem is found in the fact that people vary in the extent to which they feel this group consciousness. Some people may not feel it at all. Some identify completely with a group. The latter seldom think of themselves as anything but a member of a particular group. Still, we have a difficult time expressing this feeling because the language does not provide us with the appropriate words. There is no phrase in English that can really evoke the feeling of group unity or identity.

In considering the problem of definition in this way, we have not simply confused the issue but have, instead, discovered an important key to the analysis of nationalism as an ideology. All of the words and phrases considered relate to ties or links among individuals that go to form a new entity with which the individual can identify and toward which he can have feelings of loyalty. In nationalism, this entity is the nation or the nationality. But again the words nation and nationality are imprecise. Again it is difficult to know exactly what they mean. What is a nation? What is a nationality? Are they different from a state? From a country? Can there be more than one nationality within a nation? What is it that provides the ties that go to make up these entities?

These questions cannot be answered here, but it is possible to find workable definitions for patriotism and nationalism.

Patriotism: the more or less conscious conviction of a person that his own welfare and that of the significant groups to which he belongs are dependent upon the preservation or expansion (or both) of the power and culture of his society.

Nationalism: the set of more or less uniform demands (1) which people in a society share, (2) which arise from their patriotism, (3) for which justifications exist and can be readily expressed, (4) which incline them to make personal sacrifices in behalf of their government's aims, and (5) which may or may not lead to appropriate action.[6]

Obviously, for Doob patriotism is the basic phenomenon with nationalism as a possible product. Hence, it would appear that patriotism, as defined above, is a necessary prerequisite for the development of nationalism.

In explaining his definitions, Doob goes on to point out that patriotism as he has defined it is probably universal, but that nationalism is probably not because the demands are not always present. It is also always possible for patriotism to give rise to nationalism, particularly if the individual believes that his society is threatened. Finally, Doob says that both definitions are not historically limited, so that they refer to patriotism or nationalism at any time or place.[7] This is the type of definition that is necessary for a thorough understanding of nationalism.

Let us now examine Doob's definition more carefully so that we will have a better understanding of it, which can then be used in a general consideration of nationalism and political ideology. First, patriotism stripped of all its connotations comes down to a person's belief that his best interests are served by "the preservation or expansion (or both) of the power and culture of his society." Nationalism is sometimes popularly supposed to relate primarily to the expansion of the power of a society, but a brief glimpse at any case of nationalism illustrates Doob's point well. For example, the nationalism attributed to the developing countries is clearly not only a nationalism of power but also one of culture. Italian

---

[6] Leonard W. Doob, *Patriotism and Nationalism: Their Psychological Foundations* (New Haven, Conn.: Yale University Press, 1964), p. 6.

[7] Ibid., pp. 6–7.

nationalism under Benito Mussolini was distinctly concerned with both power and culture. For Mussolini, it was the greatness of Rome that provided his goal, and it was not only the vast territories that Rome had controlled that interested Mussolini but also the intellectual leadership it had exercised. Germany under the Nazis also stressed its great cultural tradition. All of these cases illustrate the basic feeling of patriotism that gives rise to nationalism. The demands that Doob calls nationalism have the five characteristics outlined in the definition. They must be shared, based on patriotism, have some justification that is valid to the individuals involved, produce the possibility of personal sacrifice, and lead to actions on the part of the individuals to bring about the desired goals.

Clearly, in order to understand the position encompassed by nationalism, we have to understand the feeling that Doob characterizes as patriotism before we would be capable of understanding the particular demands that he encompasses under the word *nationalism*. As was indicated earlier, our ability to understand this feeling or conviction is limited by our inability to express adequately such a feeling. Still, we must make some further attempt. Symbols of nationality such as the flag and the national anthem are supposed to produce in us a feeling akin to patriotism. It is probably true that even the most unnationalistic of us has, in fact, felt the effect of such symbols at one time or another in our lives. The effect is hard to characterize. Perhaps it is a thrill of recognition at belonging to something larger and more important than ourselves. Perhaps it is simply the feeling of belonging. Phrased another way, it might be the recognition that our destinies and our lives are wrapped up in the destinies and lives of many others. But our recognition of this comes through symbols. We cannot see in others the same thing that we can see and feel in a symbol. We respond to it emotionally; we do not think about what a bad piece of music the national anthem may be or that the flag is simply different colored cloth sewn together. We see in it and feel in it an emotion that makes us one with a community.

In this way, nationalism can act upon an individual more powerfully than any other ideology. All ideologies can affect individuals emotionally, and each ideology has certain sacred symbols that produce a reaction in the believer. But nationalism is stronger than any of these others because the symbols and signs produce the reaction sometimes even in the nonbeliever who has been conditioned from birth to react emotionally to flag, country, national anthem, and so forth.

Nationalism, being so fundamentally a thing of the emotions, is perhaps the most potent of the ideologies. It affects individuals more deeply and it needs less reinforcement than do any of the other ideologies. An individual can gain a deep, lasting commitment to a nation that cannot be changed easily. The other ideologies may become this deeply rooted within an individual, but they seem to do so less often.

The feelings that nationalism arouse have been presented and defended in many ways. Teutonic or German nationalism reached heights of emotion in the operas of Richard Wagner.[8] They appeal to, and they are built upon, deeply held feeling. In the same way, but on a less emotional level, Edmund Burke appeals to this feeling as he talks about society as a pact between those living, those dead, and those yet to be born.[9] It is, for Burke, a union among all generations that cannot be lightly changed or broken. The nation is something, for Burke, that is for all eternity. Wagner is more emotional and he presents us in his operas with the basic folk tales and myths that, to him, are the rudiments and the roots of a great German nation. It is not surprising that Adolf Hitler, who in *Mein Kampf* expresses great feeling for the German nation, was a great lover of the operas of Wagner. Hitler built national socialism on the same basic feelings and some of the same ideas that Wagner presented musically.[10]

Having looked briefly in this general way at nationalism, it would be appropriate to look at the notion of internationalism, which we indicated earlier could be considered similar to nationalism. Immediately, one notices that it does not produce the same emotional fervor as does nationalism. Internationalism seems to be something of the reason rather than the emotions. People who support internationalism argue against the feelings

---

[8] Wilhelm Richard Wagner (1813–83) is best known for his operas expressing German mythology.

[9] Edmund Burke (1729–97). A famous British politician and political philosopher. Primarily remembered as a founder of modern conservatism. See his *Reflections on the Revolution in France*, ed., Thomas H. D. Mahoney (Indianapolis, Ind.: Bobbs-Merrill, 1955), p. 110.

[10] In each of the later chapters, we will look at the ideas of a variety of nationalists. Here we stop with the general concept.

aroused by nationalism, saying that they are divisive in their impact and that they lead to innumerable dangerous confrontations between nations. Internationalists believe that the world as a whole should be in some way united. They do not all agree on what this way should be. Some, for example, argue for a world government with very strong powers. Others argue for some sort of loose confederation, and still others argue for a federal system of government similar to that of the United States, where powers would be divided between a world government and the government of each country making up the world government.

In a general sense, internationalism does partake of the same sort of phenomena that nationalism does. It requires a recognition of ties among all individuals in the world in the same sense that nationalism requires a recognition of ties among the others that live in a particular country. We noted the symbols that give rise to the feeling of nationalism. Internationalism does not have such symbols, and it is likely that an individual will seldom have an emotional identification with the world as a whole, even though he may intellectually recognize his tie to others around the world. Thus, internationalism is not likely to be as strong a force in the 20th century as nationalism is unless some crisis produces the need for these ties to be recognized and the emotional fervor that would bring about an actual identification of the individual with a world community.

Nationalism and political ideology

Every ideology of the 20th century has at some time been affected by nationalism. Every ideology of the 20th century has adapted to nationalism. Therefore, as we discuss each ideology, we shall look for the impact of nationalism on it. Nationalism is both a separate ideology and a pervading influence in many other ideologies. It is most apparent in national socialism and fascism, but it also exists in all the others. It seems that the more rational the ideology, the less immediate the impact of nationalism. But there is no ideology that escapes its impact. In this way, the 20th century is the age of nationalism.

Since the major consideration of nationalism will take place in the individual chapters on the other ideologies, this chapter has been concerned almost solely with problems of definition and an attempt to understand the meaning of nationalism. The impact of nationalism on the other ideologies will be considered in each chapter as it becomes appropriate, and the basic definition of nationalism used here, Doob's, will be used in the subsequent chapters.

At the same time, it might be useful to make a few general comments about the political implications of nationalism in today's world. The most obvious political effect of nationalism is divisiveness in the international community. We see this in Eastern Europe, where various countries have gradually split away from the domination of the Soviet Union, and in the conflict between France and Britain over the latter's entry into the Common Market. The second effect of nationalism, which might be seen as a second level of divisiveness, is found in the emerging nations of Africa and Asia and the Middle East. These nations have recognized some of the advantages of unity among themselves, but nationalism has made it impossible for them to work effectively together. In addition, feelings of nationalism have put wedges between the newly emerging nation and the older colonial power. We will look at both of these points more closely when we talk about the ideologies of the developing nations.

Finally, it should be noted that nationalism has provided a means of unifying countries.

It is a common argument among some scholars in the field of international politics that to some extent nationalism affects virtually all acts of a country in its dealings with other countries. Each country defines what is in its national interest and attempts to act as a separate unit in achieving this desired goal. Only when alliances are viewed as serving this national interest will these countries join together with others. Thus, we see a further political impact of nationalism.

We have previously discussed the impact of nationalism on the individual nationalist, but it would still be appropriate to reiterate the point briefly. The individual is emotionally affected by nationalism. This can influence him in all his perceptions of the world and of the various peoples in it. Although it can unite the individuals within a country, nationalism can separate them from individuals in other countries.

Suggested readings

Since two bibliographies are available, the following list is composed of general works on nationalism. Some further works relating nationalism to particular political ideologies will be found in the suggested readings following the other chapters.

Bibliographies

Deutsch, Karl W. *Interdisciplinary Bibliography on Nationalism 1935–1953.* Cambridge, Mass.: Technology Press, 1955.

Pinson, Koppel S. *A. Bibliographic Introduction to Nationalism.* New York: Columbia University Press, 1935.

General works

Akzin, Benjamin. *State and Nation.* London: Hutchinson University Library, 1964.

———. (ed.). *Nationalism in Asia and Africa.* New York: Meridian Books, 1970.

Baron, Salo W. *Modern Nationalism and Religion.* New York: Harper & Bros., 1947.

Carr, Edward Hallett. *Nationalism and After.* London: Macmillan & Co., 1945.

Chadwick, H. Munro. *The Nationalities of Europe and the Growth of National Ideologies.* Cambridge, Eng.: Cambridge University Press, 1945.

Deutsch, Karl W. *Nationalism and Its Alternatives.* New York: Alfred A. Knopf, 1969.

———. *Nationalism and Social Communication: An Inquiry into the Foundations of Nationality.* 2d ed. Cambridge, Mass.: M.I.T. Press, 1966.

———., and William J. Foltz (eds.). *Nation-Building.* New York: Atherton Press, 1963.

Doob, Leonard W. *Patriotism and Nationalism: Their Psychological Foundations.* New Haven, Conn.: Yale University Press, 1964.

Hayes, Carlton J. H. *Essays on Nationalism.* New York: Russell & Russell, 1966. Originally published in 1926.

———. *The Historical Evolution of Modern Nationalism.* New York: Russell & Russell, 1969. Originally published in 1931.

Hertz, Friedrich O. *Nationality in History and Politics, A Study of the Psychology and Sociology of National Sentiment and Character.* Oxford: Clarendon Press, 1944.

Janowsky, Oscar. *Nationalities and National Minorities.* New York: Columbia University Press, 1945.

Kedourie, Elie. *Nationalism.* Rev. ed. London: Hutchinson University Library, 1961.

Kohn, Hans. *The Age of Nationalism: The First Era of Global History.* New York: Harper & Bros., 1962.

————. *The Idea of Nationalism, A Study in Its Origins and Background.* New York: Collier Books, 1967. Originally published in 1944.

————. *Nationalism, Its Meaning and History.* Rev. ed. Princeton, N.J.: D. Van Nostrand, 1965.

————. *Prophets and Peoples: Studies in Nineteenth Century Nationalism.* New York: Macmillan Co., 1946.

Minogue, K. R. *Nationalism.* New York: Basic Books, 1967.

Muir, Ramsay. *Nationalism and Internationalism.* London: Constable & Co., 1916.

Rejai, Mostafa, and Enloe, Cynthia H. "Nation-State and State-Nations." *International Studies Quarterly,* 13 (June, 1969), pp. 140–58.

Royal Institute of International Affairs. *Nationalism.* London: Oxford University Press, 1939.

Shafer, Boyd C. *Nationalism, Myth and Reality.* New York: Harcourt, Brace, Jovanovich, 1955.

Snyder, Louis L. *The Meaning of Nationalism.* New Brunswick, N.J.: Rutgers University Press, 1954.

————. *New Nationalism.* Ithaca, N.Y.: Cornell University Press, 1968.

————. (ed.). *Dynamics of Nationalism: Readings in Its Meaning and Development.* New York: Van Nostrand Reinhold, 1955.

Sulzbach, Walter. *National Consciousness.* Washington: American Council on Public Affairs, 1943.

Tagore, Sir Rabindranath. *Nationalism.* New York: Macmillan Co., 1917.

Ward, Barbara. *Nationalism and Ideology.* New York: W. W. Norton & Co., 1966.

Zangwill, Israel. *The Principle of Nationalities.* London: Watts, 1917.

Znaniecki, Florian. *Modern Nationalities.* Urbana: University of Illinois Press, 1952.

3

COMMUNISM

Among the major ideologies today, the most misunderstood in the United States is communism. This is probably true at least in part because communism is the most noticeable alternative to the democratic ideology. In addition, the fact that communism is the official ideology of the Soviet Union and China, the most obvious military threats to the United States, plays an important role in the misunderstanding of communism in the United States today. Furthermore, it should be noted that there is a tremendous fear of communism in the United States. It is difficult to pin down precisely the reasons for the fear of communism in this country. It is based in part upon misunderstanding and in part on the competition between the Communist countries and the United States. It also stems from communism's opposition to capitalism and the attacks that Communist leaders make upon democratic ideology. The military posture of the world today is an additional factor, but the fear of communism has been common in the United States for most of this century, and therefore the current military situation does not adequately explain this seemingly deep-rooted fear.

Although it is not the purpose here to attempt any thoroughgoing analysis of the causes of this fear, it may help us understand some things about communism if we attempt to describe briefly some of the more obvious reasons. So far we have the following possible explanations:

1. Communist attacks on capitalism and democracy
2. The military posture in the world today

A third reason might be a belief in the Communist desire to conquer the entire world. A fourth reason might be found in a tendency to reject any group that challenges basic contemporary institutions. We shall look at some of these accepted notions regarding communism in the following pages.

There is much talk about the "Communist conspiracy" and Communist attempts to control the world. Although some justification for these beliefs can be found in Communist writings, they seem to represent a misunderstanding of contemporary communism. Based on the writings of Karl Marx (1818–83) and Friedrich Engels (1820–95),[1] as developed by N. Lenin (real name: Vladimir Ilich Ulyanov: 1870–1924) and others, communism is now the official ideology of two of the largest and most powerful countries of the world, the U.S.S.R. and China, and a number of smaller countries around them.

Many Americans make the error of simply equating the ideas of contemporary communism with those of Marx and Engels. Although it is impossible to understand communism fully as it is today without grasping the central ideas developed by Marx, Engels, and Lenin, the differences between their ideas and contemporary communism are great, and in this chapter some of the similarities and differences will be examined. There are many similar errors which distort the meaning of both Marx and Engels and contemporary communism. One of the most common of these is to view communism as being completely monolithic, allowing no national or even personal differences. Although it would undoubtedly be impossible for such total conformity to ever exist, and although it could not be further from the truth, belief in it is still widely held. The changes in Eastern Europe point to two major ways in which this view of communism as a completely monolithic system are incorrect. In the first place, the attempts of a variety of the Eastern European countries, such as Czechoslovakia, to change their systems internally while still remaining a Communist country illustrates that there are important national differences among Communist countries. This same point should also be clear to anyone viewing objectively the split between Moscow and Peking or

---

[1] For our purposes Marx and Engels can be treated as essentially the same. For a more sophisticated discussion see, Friedrich Engels, *Selected Writings,* ed., W. O. Henderson (Baltimore: Penguin Books, 1967), and Fritz Nova, *Friedrich Engels; His Contributions to Political Theory* (London: Vision Press, 1967).

the split in previous years between Russia and Yugoslavia. In addition, the response of the Soviet Union to the Czechoslovakian reforms illustrates the personal differences within one country, the Soviet Union, illustrating as it does the struggle between the proponents of Stalin and their opponents. From all of this it should be sufficiently clear that neither communism nor the Communist nations are any more monolithic than democracy and the democratic nations.

Since communism is so widespread today, it is obviously important to understand it. In order to do so, it is essential to look first at the philosophic basis of communism as found in the thought of Karl Marx and Friedrich Engels and then to turn to the developments and changes made in this basic doctrine by such thinkers as Lenin, Mao Tse-tung, Khrushchev, and others.

Philosophical basis—materialism

The basis of Marx's philosophy is found in the influence of economics on men. Although Marx did not develop this notion very thoroughly himself, he once spelled out in capsule form the fundamental thesis, saying that it ". . . served as the guiding thread in my studies." Although the jargon is a bit difficult to follow, it is still good to have this statement in Marx's own words, and it will become clearer later.

In the social production of their means of existence men enter into definite, necessary relations which are independent of their will, productive relationships which correspond to a definite state of development of their material productive forces. The aggregate of these productive relationships constitutes the economic structure of society, the real basis on which a juridical and political superstructure arises, and to which definite forms of social consciousness correspond. The mode of production of the material means of existence conditions the whole process of social, political, and intellectual life. It is not the consciousness of men that determines their existence, but, on the contrary, it is their social condition that determines their consciousness. At a certain stage of their development the material productive forces of society come into contradiction with the existing productive relationships within which they had moved before. From forms of development of the productive forces these relationships are transformed into their fetters. Then an epoch of social revolution opens. With the change in the economic foundation the whole vast superstructure is more or less rapidly transformed.[2]

---

[2] Karl Marx, "Preface," in *A Contribution to the Critique of Political Economy*, trans., N. I. Stone (Chicago: Charles H. Kerr & Co., 1913), pp. 11–12.

I have thus quoted Marx because, as I hope to show, this remarkable passage thoroughly summarizes his basic ideas.

The most basic point, which is a truism today, is that the way men think is greatly affected by the way they live. It would be very difficult today to argue against this point. As was noted in the introduction, the whole process known as socialization is the means by which an individual gains the values of his particular society. The point we made was that an individual by his position in life, economically, socially, and so forth, and by his family background, his religious preference, his educational experiences, and by such daily influences as the mass media, is presented with a picture of the world or a group of pictures of the world that help to form his basic value system. In other words, the way an individual lives does quite clearly affect the way he thinks.

But the basic point that is generally accepted today is not quite the same as the point that Marx was making. Marx argued that the forms taken by law, religion, politics, aesthetics, philosophy, and so forth, which he called the *superstructure,* are determined by the economic structure and processes of society. The key word in the discussion by Marx is the word *determined.* While making the more general point about socialization above, we were careful to always say that the way a man lives *influences* or *helps* form the way he thinks. We did not say that these things *determined* the way he thinks. In addition, it should be noted that we were careful to talk in rather broad ways about the sorts of things that influence man's developing value system. We did not, as Marx does, narrow our analysis to economics. Thus, it should be clear that Marx's position is not one that is generally accepted today at least in the non-Communist world, although no one would deny that economic factors are an important influence on man's value system. It is clear that economic factors do influence man's values and man's political behavior. If one were to tone down Marx's statement slightly to read that economic relations are one of the most important or even the most important but not the only factor that shapes men and society, it would be more acceptable today. Although we no longer accept the details of his analysis, his basic assumptions provide a way of looking at the world that leads to a much greater understanding of the forces that influence the development of man.

In its simplest form, these statements constitute Marx's materialism, and any understanding of the rest of his thought must be based on a thorough understanding of materialism. The basic notion, to which Marx adds certain complexities to be discussed later, is that all ideas, all men's thoughts, are reflections of matter or nature. Marx's position is that the material world around us, nature, determines the social, political, religious, and philosophical worlds. Marx took this idea and developed it by emphasizing economics until it formed the basis of his whole system.

In developing his materialist approach, Marx was attacking a school of German philosophy known as idealism. Its major exponent had been Georg Wilhelm Friedrich Hegel (1770–1831), and it was particularly against Hegel that Marx directed his attack. Hegel's ideas and the diverse influence they had on Marx is a complex subject and cannot be explored thoroughly here. But some attempt at explanation must be made because Hegel's influence on Marx, both in what he accepted and what he rejected, was so great. Suffice it to say that Hegel's basic proposition, from Marx's viewpoint, was the existence of an Absolute Spirit—sometimes Hegel called it God—that gradually revealed more and more of itself as higher and higher stages of freedom for man. In Hegel's philosophy the ideal and the material, or concrete, as he called it, were intimately connected, but not as cause and effect, as the material and the superstructure were related in Marx. For Hegel, the two were closely bound together, each influencing the other. Ultimately, the ideal was the more important factor for Hegel.

Marx directed his main attack on Hegel at this idealism. As Marx put it, he turned Hegel on his head by emphasizing the material rather than the ideal. Marx, of course, stressed economic relationships in his definition of the material rather than physical nature or the like. For this reason, Marx has been called an economic determinist, but the idea of materialism is not quite that simple. By stressing the material, Marx is able to argue that his position is scientific (Marx's approach is often called scientific socialism)[3] because matter, the material, is subject to objective scientific analysis and laws; it behaves in a predictable manner. Marx was one of the first men to argue that economics could also be treated scientifically, that it also followed certain laws. He generalized his materialism much further, contending that history also followed certain patterns and that these patterns could be discovered and projected into the future. Marx did not claim that he could predict the future with certainty; all he argued was that, if

---

[3] The best statement of this position is still Engels, *Socialism: Utopian and Scientific* (1880). Many editions are available.

conditions continued as they were at the present, certain things would probably happen in the future. If conditions changed, which they did (Marx had argued that they probably would not), the future would be different. Since they did change to some extent within his lifetime, some of Marx's positions changed, but he continued to believe that the basic projections he had made still held true. Finally, it must be noted that Marx believed that history was moving not only to a different stage but also to a better one. The pattern that he found in history and which he thought was a basic tool of analysis was the dialectic. Hegel, too, had argued that history was moving to different and better stages, and he also used the dialectic as his basic tool of analysis.

Dialectical materialism

Probably the most difficult addition that Marx made to materialism was the dialectic. Therefore, his position is sometimes referred to as *dialectical materialism*. The dialectic seems to have originated in Greek thought as a means of attaining truth through a process of questions and answers. In answer to an original question, such as the meaning of courage, beauty, justice, or the like, a position is stated. The questioner then criticizes this position through the question and answer process until an opposite or significantly different position is taken. Then, by a continuation of the process, an attempt is made to arrive at the true parts of both positions. The process is then continued until all are satisfied that the correct answer has been reached. The most famous illustrations of this process can be found in the dialogues of Plato, such as the *Republic*.

Marx took the dialectic from Hegel, who argued that all ideas develop through this dialectical process of thesis (first position), antithesis (second position), and synthesis (truth of the opposites), which becomes a new thesis and thus continues the process. Figure 3–1 represents the most common way of picturing the process. This illustration shows us something of what both Hegel and Marx are getting at. Starting at the bottom with the original thesis (first position), we see its "opposite" in the antithesis (second position). This opposition is not one of complete difference; it is produced from the thesis in one of two ways, spelled out in the first two laws of the dialectic.

1. *The transformation of quantity into quality.* Changes in degree gradually produce a change in quality or kind. (The usual example is the

FIGURE 3–1

The Dialectic

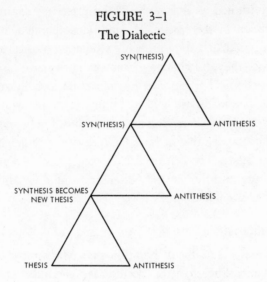

change in water from a solid (ice), to a liquid, to a gas. The changes Hegel had in mind were more basic, say H_2O to H_2O_2).

2. *Unity or identity of opposites.* Contradictions in the thesis become the antithesis. (See change of quantity into quality.) Thus, the opposites are actually one. In addition, the thesis and antithesis become unified, differently, in the synthesis.

This unification of the thesis and the antithesis is produced through the third law of the dialectic:

3. *Negation of the negation.* Contradictions continue to accumulate until another qualitative change is made and the synthesis is reached.

The synthesis, or the unity of the opposites, is a qualitative change as was the original step from the thesis to the antithesis. In other words, a new position is reached that is not simply the combination of the thesis and antithesis. In a similar way, chemists sometimes speak of synthesizing a new product from two or more products. Thus water, H_2O, is a synthesis of two parts hydrogen with one part oxygen to produce a product that is significantly different from the original components. The synthesis is then treated as a new product, and the process continues in the same manner. These three laws are often neglected or slighted by students of Marx, but, as will be seen later, they help to provide an understanding of the pattern taken by his analysis of history.

Marx did not attempt to apply the dialectic systematically to the material world. Some of his various followers, such as Engels and Lenin, have tried to view nature as changing dialectically and have spoken vaguely of scientific laws operating dialectically, but almost without exception these attempts have been fruitless and irrelevant and need not be discussed here.[4]

Historical materialism

On the other hand, Marx did apply the dialectic to his interpretation of history. Since any change in the economic system is gradually reflected in changes in the entire superstructure, Marx argued that it would be possible to interpret all of history from this perspective. He also contended that it might be possible to make some general statements about the future on the same basis. Again, it should be remembered that Marx did not say that he could predict the future. What he did say was that there were patterns in history that would in all probability continue into the future. Thus, an understanding of history should enable a scholar to argue that, if conditions remain the same, certain things were likely to take place in the future.

The major problem in discovering more precisely how Marx meant to explain all this is found in his use of economics, particularly the modes of production. Marx contended that economics is an exact science, but nowhere does he clearly define the nature of these modes of production, which are basic to an understanding of Marxian economics. It is possible to conclude that they consist of:

1. Available natural resources
2. Productive techniques
3. Organization of production (sometimes omitted)

But each of these components has certain potential problems which Marx did not always avoid. The first component is complicated by one of the most confusing points in Marxism, the role assigned to man's mind in the

---

[4] The student who is interested in these attempts should consult the following works: Friedrich Engels, *Anti-Dühring: Herr Eugen Dühring's Revolution in Science*, Part I, any edition; Engels, *Dialectics of Nature*, any edition; and V. I. Lenin, *Materialism and Empirio-Criticism; Critical Comments on a Reactionary Philosophy*, chap. v, any edition.

process of forming knowledge. Many natural resources are readily available to us everyday, but without the knowledge of how to use them, they are not, in fact, available. For example, uranium was not a useful natural resource until very recently. Thus, it would seem that some knowledge must be gained before any natural resources are available to man, and, if this is true, Marx's whole analysis could break down at the very beginning.

For example, if one assumed some beginning point to man, some point when he had no modes of production, it is difficult to see how he could ever develop them without the use of his mind. Although this problem was not of direct concern to Marx, it helps to illustrate the point. When man first appeared on the scene, whenever or however that came about, he would be faced with a vast abundance of natural wealth, but he would have no idea what to do with it and would die of starvation within a few days. Since this does not seem to have happened, either Marx's analysis is wrong or there must be some possible solution that would allow us to at least tentatively accept Marx's position. There seem to be two possible solutions of the problem. If we assume that man is a result of a long evolutionary process from some unknown origin, it would be possible to argue that primitive man was much more a creature of instinct than man as we know him today; and we know that instinct, however originally developed, can be extremely complex. The author once watched a young squirrel who had lived inside an apartment from the time it was a few days old go through the motions of burying some food, a piece of tomato, in the middle of the rug. After completing the motions, perhaps acting out some instinctual process, it was completely satisfied even though the tomato remained in full view. It might thus be possible to argue that some instinctual pattern might be the original mode of production.

A second solution can be found without making quite such a difficult set of assumptions. It is possible to argue that primitive man originally learned through a process of trial and error, the results of which were maintained in tribal taboos and ceremonies, such as the complex rituals found in even highly developed early agricultural societies that were supposed to determine the correct times for planting and harvesting. The first step in this process, trial and error, could be viewed as a mode of production and the problem would be solved. Some such solution or combination of solutions seems to provide a possible answer to the dilemma, although it certainly would be foolish to assume that we have or can have any idea what actually did happen.

All of this is extremely hypothetical, and it should be clearly noted that Marx's concern was with developed modes of production not with the origins of society; but it allows us to move on to the second component. As man gains in knowledge of the uses to which natural resources can be put, his mode of production changes, and he begins to develop tools and processes of manufacture. He begins to produce pottery or weave baskets; he learns to form metals into tools and weapons. These changes in turn lead to further changes in both the mode of production and the superstructure. All this is, of course, true only if man's mind plays some sort of active role in the process. The key here to Marx's analysis depends in large part on our perception of the process as opposed to Marx's. We believe that such developments and changes must come about through the learning of certain techniques and then changing them through a conscious search for better ways of doing things. In essence, we are seeing the situation from the point of view of the individual, whereas Marx is looking for an historical process.

Certainly, it is possible to maintain that a historical process is merely the accumulation of changes wrought by individuals, but we should first try to understand Marx's position before arguing with it. Here Marx is making a very simple point. He is saying that changes in productive techniques are brought about because previous changes were made. In other words, each development sets the stage for a further development. Finally, he is also saying that major changes in productive techniques, such as, for example, from herding to agriculture, produce major changes in the organization of the society involved and in the belief system of that society. In the case cited, he is obviously right; whether he continues to be right in all cases is another matter. Although the change from herding to agriculture is an obvious case where major changes in productive techniques do change the organization of society, and specifically the political system of that society, Marx is probably correct in assuming that *any* such major change does produce a major change in the society. It is again obviously true that the change from a predominantly agricultural society to a predominantly industrial society has produced many far-reaching changes in contemporary society, and there are many who argue that similar far-reaching changes will come about as production becomes more and more highly automated.

The third factor, organization of production, is the most complex one since, if it refers to the organization of industry or the like, it must be viewed as part of the superstructure rather than of the modes of production. When Marx means simply the labor applied through tools to the natural resources, there is no problem. The problem is found in the phrase "the organization of production" because our contemporary connotations connected with the word *organization* imply a structure of some sort or a system of interrelated individuals that comprise a social unit. If this were true, this would clearly refer to part of the superstructure, but what Marx seems to have meant by the phrase "the organization of production," which kept it from being part of the superstructure, is contained in the word "production." This implies that Marx is talking about labor and specifically of labor using tools to produce goods and not the way in which industry is organized.

It is possible to say with some confidence that normally Marx is talking about labor when he speaks of the organization of production, but it can be said with equal confidence that sometimes he seems to mean something like the organization of industry. When he means the latter, he is obviously being inconsistent because the organization of industry is clearly one part of the superstructure. This illustrates one of the major problems of the modes of production as determining factors in history—they are not clearly or consistently defined.

Part of the superstructure produced by the modes of production is a set of *relations of production* or property relations. These constitute the second key to Marx's theory of history. Property relations in Marx's terminology refer to the ownership of the means of production, land, property, and so on. These property relations change more slowly than do the modes of production, and therefore a conflict is formed which can only be solved by a change in the property relations. This point is important for an understanding of Marx's analysis of the changes in history and for his criticism of contemporary society. Marx argued that property relations tend to evolve much more slowly than modes of production, and property relations will have a tendency not to change to meet changing needs. Since his analysis clearly states that property relations are a product of the modes of production, it is clear that it is the property relations that must change to meet the new modes of production rather than the reverse. But, in the meantime, there is a tension between the modes of production and the property relations that is unresolved and cannot be resolved until the more slowly changing property relations have in fact changed.

This tension produces conflict within society and may in fact be one of the major reasons for the coming of a possible revolution and of Marx's certainty that the proletariat in that particular case would win the revolution. He is saying that in a given case the owners of property will not be willing to give up their ownership, even though such a change is dictated by a change in the modes of production. At the same time, they ultimately must give up such property ownership because of the change in the modes of production. Hence, one can see in operation the three laws of the dialectic mentioned before. There is the transformation of quantity into quality in the changes in the modes of production. There is the unity of opposites in the growing contradiction between the economic foundation and the superstructure. And, finally, there is the negation of the negation in arriving at the new synthesis of modes of production and superstructure.

At this point, it should be clear that, although the form of Marx's interpretation of history is dialectical, and further that the three laws of the dialectic help to illustrate the progression of his interpretation, the same analysis could be accomplished without the dialectic. In addition, Marx uses the dialectic in his conception of the progression to higher and higher or better and better stages of society. This, in essence, is the idea of progress or the notion that man and society are inevitably moving on to better things. Again, it should be noted that the dialectic is not necessary to express the idea of progress, but it is the method Marx used. An extremely popular idea in Marx's time, the idea of progress has fallen somewhat into disrepute today. Marx's use of the idea of progress is worthy of some further consideration, even though the idea of progress is not as important in contemporary thought as it was in Marx's day.

Although it would not be appropriate to go into the complexities of the idea of progress, it should be understood that it was not simply the notion of the world getting better and better every day in every way. Of course, some theorists of the idea of progress did believe that the world was constantly getting better and that man had nothing to do with whether or not the world would improve. They argued that the world was moving in a straight line from some early beginning in primitivism to some ultimate utopia or millenium in which everything would be good and beautiful. They believed that all man had to do was to wait and things would get better. But most of the believers in the idea of progress did not accept this simple formulation but developed a somewhat modified notion. It included the idea that the world, although improving, constantly fell away from the line of progress into some sort of corruption and then only by great effort, perhaps a revolution, was the world able to be brought back onto the correct path.

This point raises a second consideration in the idea of progress, that is, that the path taken by the world in its gradual betterment could be affected both for good and evil by man. Marx seemed to have assumed, as did most of the other theorists of the idea of progress, that the world would gradually get better in spite of whatever man happened to do. But, at the same time, he contended that man could improve himself and the world as a whole through concerted action. Thus, the dialectic, left to itself, would improve man's position, but knowledgeable men, such as Marx, were in a position to recognize the direction that must be taken in order to improve man's position. The importance of this point in Marx will become apparent as we discuss Lenin's theory of the Communist party.

The class struggle

An important key to an understanding of Marxism is the concept of the *class struggle*. The class struggle is a new hypothesis that Marx felt explained the period in which he lived. The class struggle is based on the contradiction between the modes of production and the relations of production just mentioned. It is this contradiction that produces the class struggle. Marx contended that in the mid-19th century the means of production were controlled by a class he called the *bourgeoisie*. This class did little if any work, but reaped immense profits from its control of the means of production. The actual labor was done by a class Marx called the *proletariat*. The mode of production required the proletariat, but it did not, according to Marx, require the bourgeoisie. Therefore, a struggle between these two classes results. Each wished to control the means of production. For Marx there was no question concerning the result—the proletariat was necessary, the bourgeoisie was not. Although he, and later Marxists, did attempt to apply the theory of the class struggle to all history, he argued that the best example of it existed in the mid-19th century in which society was clearly split into these two classes, the bourgeoisie or the capitalists, and the proletariat or the laboring class.

It is important at the outset to be very clear regarding the nature of classes and of these two classes in particular. Classes are economic in nature and are groups of men ordered according to their relationship to the nonhuman powers of production and each other. The proletariat is the class that makes its living from the sale of its labor power. The bourgeoisie or capitalist class consists of the owners of the productive resources upon which the proletariat works. This class makes its living primarily from profit, interest, and rent, although it may earn some of its income from wages paid for managerial work and for the coordination of risk-taking ventures.

Many other smaller classes existed, but they were irrelevant to the unfolding conflict. In addition, Marx had a few problems with the manner in which he included certain groups within the class system. For example, he was always unclear as to exactly where the peasantry would fit within his system. He often included the peasantry in a group loosely known as the *petite bourgeoisie* because they were landowners. At other times he split his definition of the peasantry into a variety of groups ranging from the bourgeoisie to the proletariat, but he was never clear as to exactly where to place the group of peasantry who owned their land and worked it themselves. This problem of classification has plagued Marxist theorists ever since. No one is ever quite clear where to place the peasant. In addition to the peasantry, Marx also added another class at the bottom of his classification scheme called the *lumpenproletariat,* which was composed of the dregs of society, primarily thieves, bums, and the like. Marx never made clear whether it would be possible ever to include this group within the proletariat itself, but one would assume from his writings that he did think that at some point after the revolution it would be possible to incorporate the *lumpenproletariat* into the proletariat in the same way that the bourgeoisie was to be incorporated.[5] It should be kept in mind, though,

---

[5] For discussion of these problems see John Plamenatz, *Man and Society: A Critical Examination of Some Important Social and Political Theories from Machiavelli to Marx* (London: Longmans Green & Co., 1963), vol. II, pp. 293–300, and David Mitrany, *Marx Against the Peasant: A Study in Social Dogmatism* (New York: Collier Books, 1961).

that for Marx the most important classes were the proletariat and the bourgeoisie.

The class struggle can be seen through the three laws of the dialectic. The development of industrialization produced the bourgeoisie and proletariat. These classes, although originally unified because they were for a time both necessary for the development of industrialization, become more antagonistic until they become thesis and antithesis. This is partially the effect of the growing wealth of the bourgeoisie combined with the growing poverty of the proletariat and partially the effect of the gradual failure of capitalism. Thus, we have the transformation of quantity into quality and the unity of opposites. The split gradually widens until it becomes intolerable, and we reach the negation of the negation, which produces a social revolution, and the synthesis is reached. This dialectical change must, of course, be seen as part of the broader conflict between modes of production and the property relations through which they are experienced.

Marx's criticism of capitalism

The Marxian analysis of society and the forces operating in it is directed at a commentary on, and condemnation of, industrial capitalism. Marx attributed most of the ills of contemporary society to the capitalist system and its product, the class struggle. There is no question that there were many evils inherent in developing industrialism, and certainly Marx was not the only one to point them out. His comments on contemporary society are interesting, though, because they indicate a great deal about Marx and the way he viewed the world. In addition, both Marxian communism and contemporary communism are attempts to solve the problems of industrialism. Much of the thrust and appeal of Marxism is found in these criticisms of the workings of the industrial system. Therefore, a thorough understanding of communism is impossible without a careful consideration of these criticisms.

Obviously, since economics is the foundation of the entire social system, Marx's economic criticisms should be considered first. The primary points in Marxian economics are the *labor theory of value*, the doctrine of *subsistence wages*, and the theory of *surplus value*. Generally, Marx used value in the sense of real costs in labor. Nothing else was considered. In other words, the value, not the price, of any manufactured object was based on the amount of labor time consumed in producing it. This is the labor theory of value. A man has to work a certain number of hours or days to produce enough to provide him with a living. Marx assumed that the capitalist would pay the man only enough to keep him alive, a subsistence wage. Marx made this assumption because:

1. There was a surplus of laborers and there was no need to pay more.
2. He could not conceive of the capitalist paying more than absolutely necessary.
3. He assumed that the capitalist would be faced with a series of economic crises which would make it impossible for the capitalist to pay more.

In addition, Marx believed that the profit of the capitalist was taken from the amount produced over and above the wages paid the worker. This is the theory of surplus value and can be used to explain more fully the doctrine of subsistence wages. As the capitalist replaced workers with machines, he would have to reduce wages to keep up his rate of profit, since profit came only from surplus value extracted from labor. Obviously, this is one of Marx's weakest points, but our purpose at the moment is to understand Marx, not to criticize him.

Hence, Marx's major economic criticisms of the society in which he lived turned on the exploitation of the majority, the proletariat, by the minority, the bourgeoisie. His concern was not purely economic but was centered on the extent to which the system kept proletarians from ever fulfilling their potentials as individuals. It was impossible for them to move up in society in any way. They were denied education and were thus kept from any real understanding of their deplorable position.

The state was the tool of the dominant class, the bourgeoisie, and was used by them to suppress violently any attempt by the proletariat to better themselves. It should be kept in mind that the state to Marx and many other radical theorists of the day referred to all those official persons, such as the police, the army, and so forth, that could be and were used to suppress the workers. In addition, Marx contended that as long as the bourgeoisie was the dominant class, the government would be its tool and could not be made responsive to the needs of other classes. The state or the government was always viewed by Marx as the tool of the dominant class, whichever class that might be, and it would so remain as long as there was more than one class. The state, for many radicals of the period and for certain radicals today, has become the epitome of evil, the symbol of all that is bad about society. This is particularly true among the anarchists, and, when we discuss anarchists in detail, this will be explored further. It is also true of Marx and some of Marx's followers, particularly prior to Lenin. This notion probably developed because so often the state in the bureaucracy, in the police, and in the army represents all the forces seemingly opposed to the workers. The history of the labor movement in the United States, for example, illustrates frequent use of the police, the army, and such institutions as the National Guard to put down strikes, and in general to oppose the labor movement. It is easy to see, then, why the state could come to symbolize all those forces opposed to the worker or even to change itself. Thus, Marx's ultimate utopia, Full Communism, has no state. And in this he is similar to the anarchists.

The religious system was also in the hands of the bourgeoisie, and Marx held that it was used to convince the proletariat that if they obeyed the state and their bosses they would be rewarded in another life. This is what Marx meant by his famous statement that religion is the opium of the people. The proletarian was lulled into accepting his way of life by the vision of heaven. This life might well be harsh, but, if he just stood it for a brief time, he would be rewarded in the next life. Marx felt that this kept the workers from actively seeking to change the system. In this way, the religious system was a major focus of Marx's criticisms of contemporary society. He saw what he believed to be the superstition and hocus-pocus of religion used by the dominant class, the bourgeoisie, to hold the proletariat in its downtrodden position. Thus, Marx made many scathing attacks at the religious system of his day and argued that the future society in which the proletariat would rule would have no need for religion. It should also be noted that Marx's materialist position was diametrically opposed to any idea of religion.

As was noted earlier, the state and the religious system were both part of what Marx called the superstructure. They were not fundamental economic structures of society. Essentially, they were a reflection of the property relations and would change as these property relations changed. Thus, as the class antagonisms were overcome during the dictatorship of the proletariat both the state and religion would begin to disappear.

The capitalist system degraded the worker in all of his relationships. Since he had to fight constantly against others of his class for bare subsistence, he could never hope to establish any sort of valid relationship with another person. For example, Marx wrote bitterly of the effect that capitalism had on marriage and the family. To Marx, the family system of his day was a repetition of the class struggle. The husband symbolized the bourgeoisie, the wife, the proletariat. The contemporary marriage system under capitalism was monogamy supplemented by adultery and prostitution, and it could not change until capitalism ceased to exist. The contemporary marriage system had originated as an institution of private property at about the same time that private property in land and goods had originated. It developed in order to insure that a man's property would be handed on to his sons. The only way this could be done was to endow the sons of one woman with a particular legal status. This in no way limited the man's relationships with other women; it supposedly limited the wife's relationships with other men. In practice, as shown by adultery, this latter proscription did not work. It failed because of what Marx called "individual sex-love." He believed that sometime after the development of monogamous marriage, there developed the tendency to find one sex-love partner and no other. This could, of course, occur after marriage, and it explained the existence of adultery. But, as will be seen later, it also provided Marx with the basis for the true monogamous marriage that would develop after the revolution.[6]

Revolution[7]

This revolution was supposed to develop as a result of the series of crises that capitalism was to experience. They failed to appear as regularly or as seriously as Marx had expected, and thus the revolution did not develop in the way Marx expected. In a little book entitled, *Imperialism; the Highest Stage of Capitalism,* Lenin attempted to show why these crises failed to occur as expected. Lenin argued that by colonizing and exploiting underdeveloped countries, the capitalists were temporarily able to stave off these crises. Colonial exploitation made it possible to pay the workers slightly better by providing the capitalists with:

1. Cheap raw materials

---

[6] Engels discussed the family at length in *The Origin of the Family, Private Property, and the State* (New York: International Publishers, Co., n.d.).

[7] Here we leave Marx temporarily and turn to his followers.

2. Cheap labor
3. Markets for manufactured goods and excess capital

Imperialism merely postpones the revolution; it is not a permanent solution. But it may lull the proletariat into believing that revolution will not be necessary.[8] Therefore, Lenin and Mao Tse-tung developed means for fomenting and directing a successful revolution.

In discussing the Marxian approach to revolution, it is instructive to distinguish between two different types of revolution—the political and the social. The political revolution takes place when political power is seized by the proletariat. The social revolution takes place, first, through changes made in the property relations of society and, second, as the superstructure adjusts to these changes.

The political revolution is only the preparatory stage for the much more important social revolution. As the state is the tool of the dominant class, it becomes the tool of the proletariat when the economic system is changed and the superstructure adjusts to the change. Finally, the state disappears as the social revolution is completed.

Marx usually saw the political revolution as violent, although he did allow for the possibility of peaceful change. The revolution would probably be violent for two reasons. First, Marx argued that achieving the synthesis would always be sudden; thus the gradualness implicit in peaceful change was ruled out by the dialectic. Second, the bourgeoisie would never agree to its disappearance as a class and would force the proletariat into a violent revolution. In addition, Marx believed that revolution was good and necessary and worked for it himself.

Lenin's contribution was the development of the revolutionary party, which was an organizational weapon in the struggle to overthrow capitalism. Lenin argued that a party was necessary because the proletariat was incapable of recognizing its role as the revolutionary class whereas the party provided this necessary consciousness. As Alfred G. Meyer put it, "The party is conceived as the organization, incarnation, or institutionalization of class consciousness."[9] The party would be made up of those who

---

[8] Alfred G. Meyer provides an excellent analysis of Lenin's theory of imperialism and its implications. See chaps. xi and xii of *Leninism* (New York: Frederick A. Praeger, 1962).

[9] Ibid., pp. 32–33.

had achieved this consciousness and had also become professional revolutionists. In the popular phrase, the party was to be the "vanguard of the
proletariat"; it would point the way and lead the proletariat to its goal.

The party was to be the mechanism for spurring man on to the higher
stage of progress that we mentioned earlier in discussing the dialectic as an
expression of the idea of progress. Since the idea of progress includes the
possibility of an individual or a group or some institution helping to move
the world on to a higher plane, it is clear that within Communist ideology,
this role was to be fulfilled by the party. The party, "the vanguard of the
proletariat," was to be the instrument that would be used to insure continued progress. It would bring together the divided masses of workers,
and it would express what they were truly feeling but were incapable of
expressing. It would mold them and unify them and make them into a
force for change to something better. They would be the vehicle to overcome the conservatism of the property owners who had become outmoded,
and they would, perhaps through a revolution, remove the property from
the hands of its current owners and redistribute it through the mechanism
of the party. Thus, the party would fulfill a key role at this point in bringing together the disparate masses into a working unified group that would
be able to move society on to a higher plane.

It should be kept in mind that the proletarians as individual members
of a class would not be likely to recognize their historic role. In the first
place, they would be much too busy attempting to stay alive to be concerned with class questions. Second, very few would ever identify themselves as class members. Thus, it would be left up to the few who become
aware, the party members, to prepare for the great role the proletariat
would play.

The importance of Lenin's party is found in the idea of the professional
revolutionary and in the organizational principle, democratic centralism.
Although the party would be composed of a small conspiratorial group of
professional revolutionists, Lenin believed that it should develop contacts
throughout the society as a whole, since no revolution could be successful
without the support of, or at least little direct opposition from, the largest
part of the population of the country. This meant that the party members
would have to have a variety of organizational skills. They would have to
be experts at agitation and propaganda. Since they had to be able to establish and maintain a vast network of "front" organizations throughout

the country, they would have to be expert administrators. Ideally, prior to the revolution, the majority of the population should be organized into a variety of these groups which would also provide the basis for organization once the revolution has succeeded. In addition, the party member would have to prepare constantly for the revolution, since it would come only when the masses suddenly revolted against their oppressors.

Ideally, the party might light the spark[10] that set the masses afire, but the spark might come anywhere, anytime, and the party had to be in readiness to ride the revolution into power. It is clear that Lenin believed that it was possible for the party to produce the necessary conditions for a revolution, but it is equally clear that he believed that it was impossible to be absolutely sure when the revolution would come. Hence, the party must always be prepared for the revolution coming at an unexpected, perhaps even an unpropitious, time.

The principle of organization that would make all this possible is democratic centralism. This principle combines freedom of discussion with centralized control and responsibility. Before any decision is made by the party, there should be complete freedom to dissent; after the decision is made, it must be accepted unanimously. Lenin felt that this principle could function adequately, since the party members started from a position of agreement regarding goals. In practice, freedom of discussion was often forgotten. Democratic centralism would also serve as the principle of organization in the period immediately following the revolution, and this will be discussed more completely later.

As a technique of revolutionary organization, democratic centralism has important characteristics that must not be overlooked. If one is planning a revolution, one must be very careful to organize one's followers in such a way that they can be brought into action at a moment's notice. They must also be able to be brought into action in a completely concerted manner without disagreements or squabbles over what is to be done now and what is to be done later, or arguments about the correct techniques of taking over the government or who is to do this or that at a particular moment. It is absolutely essential that there be complete agreement among the revolutionists over the techniques of the revolution and the organization of

---

[10] The theory of the spark is important for Lenin. One of his newspapers was called *The Spark (Iskra)*, and he often refers to the necessity of some incident igniting the masses.

society immediately after the successful revolution. Democratic centralism provides this by giving the leaders complete control over the actions of the revolutionists while at the same time allowing all members of the party to participate freely and openly in the process of reaching the appropriate decisions.

Other Marxist theorists have also contributed to the techniques of revolution. For example, Mao Tse-tung's theory of guerrilla warfare is also an organizational weapon. Mao's theory can be divided into two parts, the strictly military principles and some political principles that are derived from one of the military principles. The military principles are as follows:

1. Attack dispersed, isolated enemy forces first; attack concentrated strong enemy forces later.
2. Take small and medium cities and extensive rural areas first; take big cities later.
3. Make the wiping out of the enemy's effective strength our main objective; do not make holding or seizing a city or place our main objective.
4. In every battle to concentrate an absolutely superior force . . . to encircle the enemy forces completely, strive to wipe them out thoroughly and do not let any escape from the net.
5. Fight no battle unprepared, fight no battle if we are not sure of winning. . . .
6. Give full play to our style of fighting—courage in battle, no fear of sacrifice, no fear of fatigue, and continuous fighting (that is, fighting successive battles in a short time without rest).
7. Strive to wipe out the enemy through mobile warfare. At the same time, pay attention to the tactics of positional attack and capture enemy fortified points and cities.
8. With regard to attacking cities, resolutely seize all enemy fortified points and cities which are weakly defended.
9. Replenish our strength with all the arms and most of the personnel captured from the enemy.
10. Make good use of the intervals between campaigns to rest, train, and consolidate our troops.[11]

This last point requires a territorial base where the guerrillas will be virtually free from attack so that they will be able to rest, train, and so on. In

---

[11] Mao Tse-tung, *Selected Works* (Peking: Foreign Language Press, 1961), vol. IV, pp. 161–62. Only the main points have been stated. Mao qualified his arguments with comments on tactics for the later period when the guerrilla force has gained greatly in strength.

order to achieve this, they must have the positive support of the people in that area. This support is gained by:

1. Establishing a peasant government
2. Allowing the peasants to redistribute the land
3. Helping the peasants in whatever rebuilding activities they undertake

The territorial base will thus provide food, manpower, and, perhaps most importantly, experience in organization. Thus, Mao's theory of guerrilla warfare basically fulfills the same functions as Lenin's theory of the revolutionary party. Mao's approach to revolution is of growing importance today, and therefore it is important to recognize that the tactics outlined above are designed with the same purposes in mind as were Lenin's tactics.

The theory of the revolution is primarily concerned with tactics, not philosophy, although many of the purely tactical questions are important for understanding the underlying theory. Probably the most outstanding issue is the one of violence versus nonviolence. Historically, violence has been virtually the sole answer, even though Marx had argued that it might not be essential. More recently, the whole point of revolution has been toned down by many, but not all, Marxist theorists. Contemporary Marxist theorists of the more conservative approach argue that violent revolution may not be necessary or desirable except, perhaps, in the developing countries, and even there it may not be required. This argument rests on a number of assumptions:

1. Revolution may not be possible in most developed countries.
2. The developing countries may be more easily convinced by examples of rapid economic growth than by violence.
3. Revolutionary forms may not be readily exportable.[12]
4. Contemporary revolutions are often more nearly nationalist than Communist.

For all these reasons the tactics are changing. The extremist Marxists, often followers of Mao Tse-tung, are not convinced. They contend that the rejecton of revolution is a rejection of Marx and Engels and cannot be accepted. They are usually particularly concerned with the developing

---

[12] See Regis Debray, *Revolution in the Revolution? Armed Struggle and Political Struggle in Latin America*, trans., Bobbye Ortiz (New York: Monthly Review Press, 1967).

countries and contend that the leaders of these countries, although not usually traditional capitalists, must be replaced by Communists. Although this may not require a revolution, it is likely that this will be the only way the proletariat will be able to gain power.

One of the peculiarities of the developing nations that causes problems for the Marxist theorist is the lack of a proletariat. This was first faced by Lenin in Russia. It was true in China at the time of the Communist revolution, and Mao attempted to base his revolutionary techniques on the peasants as a revolutionary class rather than the proletariat. Nevertheless, it is usually argued that the proletariat is the most revolutionary class, even in the developing countries where the proletariat is either nonexistent or exists only in very small numbers. And if a revolution is successful without a proletariat, as it was in China, much effort is put into developing a proletarian class immediately after the revolution. This, of course, is necessary anywhere in the world today because, without a large laboring class, industrialization is impossible. Therefore, a dictatorship of the proletariat is introduced, even where the proletariat is virtually nonexistent.

This problem of the lack of the proletariat in many developing nations, or at least of a proletariat in the industrial sense that Marx usually used the term, does cause serious problems for the Marxist theorist who is attempting to discuss the developing nations. The problem is not so much in the period of the revolution, although supposedly the proletariat should lead the revolution. It is partially a theoretical, and partially a very practical, problem after the revolution. The developing nations, without exception, wish to industrialize. They cannot, in fact, industrialize without the development of an industrial proletariat. Therefore, for the theoretical reasons of the Marxian ideology which requires a proletariat, and the very practical reason of the desire and need for industrialization, one of the first steps that any Marxist leader in a developing country takes is to develop or attempt to develop a proletariat.

Dictatorship of the proletariat

After the revolution, Marx envisioned a brief transitional period known as the dictatorship of the proletariat. This stage was to be characterized by the consolidation of the power of the proletariat through the gradual disappearance of the bourgeoisie and the minor classes as they became part of the proletariat. Marx did not envision the physical destruction of the bourgeoisie and the minor classes that took place in the Soviet Union primarily under Stalin. Marx viewed the dictatorship of the proletariat as a period in which these classes would be incorporated into the proletariat by making them laborers, not by destroying them. In other words, the bourgeoisie and the other classes would be given jobs that would, over time, change their outlook on life and make them good members of the proletariat. This would be the period in which the entire superstructure would slowly change to adjust to the socialist mode of production. Loosely, the dictatorship of the proletariat should have the following characteristics:

1. Distribution of income according to labor performed.
2. Gradual disappearance of classes.
3. The state in the hands of the proletariat.
4. Increasing productivity.
5. Increasing socialist consciousness—people work with few incentives.
6. Increasing equality.
7. A command economy.
8. The economy managed by the state.

All of these characteristics were supposed to be changing fairly rapidly and the dictatorship of the proletariat was to be very brief. In practice, no country that has followed Marx's ideas has yet moved beyond the dictatorship of the proletariat. A number of countries in the world today are in what they call the dictatorship of the proletariat. Contrary to Marx, this "transitional" period does not seem to focus on the economic system. One could almost say that the dictatorship of the proletariat as practiced is based on the political system with all else as superstructure rather than being based on the economic system.

Within the political system, the central position is held by the Communist party. This is true for two reasons, both of which derive from Lenin. First, the Communist party is defined as the vanguard of the proletariat, and in any state governed by the proletariat it should automatically rule. Second, Lenin and the Communist party successfully took power in the first Communist revolution and established all of the machinery of government. Thus, the Communist party formed the government and might be expected to run it.

The major function of any political system is to integrate or pull together the country into one functioning unit and to maintain order. For these purposes, it is given broad coercive powers to help insure that its orders are carried out. The Communist party does not technically hold these powers itself, but in effect it acts as the government in most cases. In so acting, it requires an organization that has contacts throughout the entire society. In many ways, this is a carry-over of Lenin's theory of a party which would ideally touch upon the great mass of the people or the entire people through a wide variety of mass organizations, each organized on the same basis and each intimately connected with the party. The principle of organization, which has been touched upon before, is *democratic centralism*. In operation, democratic centralism acts to provide channels of information for the leadership and as a means of relaying directions throughout the country and insuring that the directions are followed. (Figures 3–2 and 3–3 illustrate the typical organization of a Communist party and its position in society.) It should also be recalled that Lenin's theory of the party included the idea that the top leadership in the party

FIGURE 3–2

Organization of a Communist Party

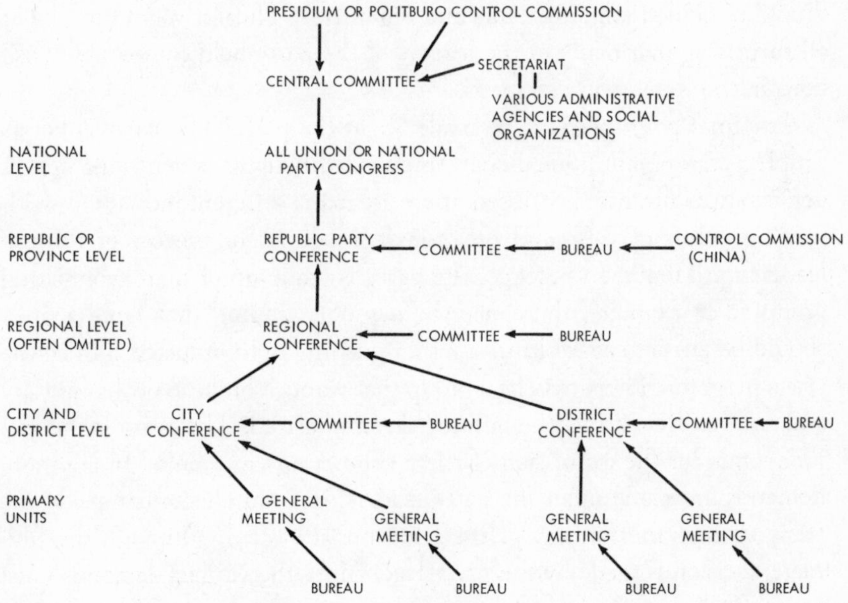

FIGURE 3–3

The Communist Party and the Society

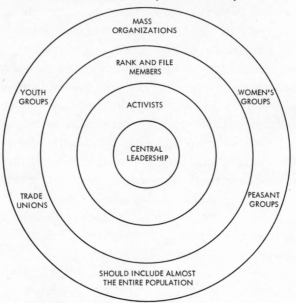

should be skilled administrators and organizers. Thus, it should not be at all surprising that many of the leaders of the party hold comparable positions in the state administration.

One final point needs to be made about the party. The party is not as simple as the organizational chart implies. Although the centralist side of democratic centralism is stressed, there are many different individuals with varying points of view and programs competing for the ear of the top leadership. Hence, in practice, the party is made up of many competing groups. For example, there may be a group arguing that more money should be put into agriculture, another pushing light industry, a third the space program. There may be a group that wants a buildup of the military and another that wants the military de-emphasized. The party is the major avenue for the expression of these competing viewpoints. In addition, demands are made upon the party leadership from elements outside the party such as the military or the educational system. Although the ultimate decision is made by the party leadership, the various demands must be carefully sorted out and assigned priorities. None can be completely neglected for long, or a section of the society and probably a section of the party itself will become disillusioned with the leadership, as happened with Khrushchev. Thus, the party appears to be monolithic, but this is only partially correct and is a much too simplified picture of the operation of the party.

One of the major concerns that has split the party has been economic planning, which is the core of the economic system. As would be expected, the party plays the determining role in establishing the economic goals and priorities. Without going into great detail about the process or the administrative organizations involved, the economic system operates as follows. Detailed data is collected from throughout the country regarding the available resources and productive capacity and the minimum needs of each area of the economy. Political decisions are made determining what to produce. This is the key decision. It is only possible to produce so much within a given period, and this means that, if the greatest emphasis is placed on consumer goods, heavy industry may have to be slighted. Some sort of balance must be reached that will fulfill the minimum needs in each area. Beyond this essential minimum the party decides what part or parts of the economy will be stressed, and the planners allocate the raw materials and set quotas accordingly. This is the meaning of a command economy managed by the state. Each industry, each agricultural section, is told what to produce and in what amounts.

A command economy means that the distribution of agricultural and manufactured goods is also centrally controlled. Usually there is some flexibility in this, and there are often open markets where some agricultural goods and craft work is sold. The distribution of income is also controlled by the state, and, in the period of the dictatorship of the proletariat, this is done according to work performed so that there is room for flexibility here, too, and there is no attempt at any leveling of income.

China is making a change in this system that has far-reaching implications for the entire social system. This is the introduction of the *commune system*. Basically, the commune system is a means of economic organization for the most efficient use of manpower, but it also is a means of political control and, the Chinese say, a step beyond the dictatorship of the proletariat. A rural commune is formed by abandoning a few villages in an area and bringing the people together into one large village. Thus, because they are not so spread out, the people are easier to control, and there is a fairly large pool of labor that can be readily shifted from agriculture to road building to dike repair as the seasons change and need arises. The urban commune is organized in a similar manner by taking all the workers from a particular factory or industry.

The commune is not merely an economic organization. It is a miniature state even though it is not self-governing. At the beginning, men, women, and children were separated in an attempt to break up the old family system, but this was rapidly changed and the nuclear family of husband and wife, children, and possibly grandparents is the basis of the commune. During the day the children are either cared for by the older women in nurseries or go to school. Other women prepare food for the entire commune, and common dining halls are the rule. Thus, many women are freed from child care and household duties to join the men in the fields or in some other work. The Chinese claim that the commune system is the basis for the new society to come after the dictatorship of the proletariat, and therefore they spend a great deal of time and effort in educating the members of the communes and the rest of the population in the great advantages that supposedly come with commune life.

According to Marx the dictatorship of the proletariat is a period of transition from the old, bad society to a new, good one. Previously, we have briefly glanced at Marx's picture of society under capitalism. Now, let us see to what extent the dictatorship of the proletariat has corrected the evils that Marx saw in capitalist society. In the first place, religion is rapidly disappearing. In the Soviet Union, religion is tolerated and is fairly free except that it cannot run schools. In China, there has never been a great emphasis on religion, but the old philosophical and ethical systems, such as Confucianism and Taoism, and the fairly small religious groups are being abolished. The family is much the same as described in the Chinese commune, except that, outside of the commune, women are not free from housework. There are, though, state-run nurseries which free women from child care, and there is a great concern with the entire socialization system.

This is illustrated by the fact that the major change under the dictatorship of the proletariat has been in education. From earliest childhood in the nurseries through widespread adult education, there is a concentrated effort to raise the educational level of the entire population while at the same time teaching the values of the new social system. In undertaking this immense task, all the available means of mass communication are being used in addition to the more traditional classroom techniques. In China in particular, the individual is constantly surrounded by propaganda broadcast over loudspeakers on the corner, in trains, in the factories, and in the fields.

In addition, most individuals are members of one or more of the mass organizations, such as labor unions or youth groups. This is a carry-over from the system of democratic centralism and its stress on involving the entire society in the revolution through a wide variety of mass organizations. These groups are comparable to the same sort of informal or formal private organizations that exist in the United States and other countries—the various fraternal organizations; organizations such as the Boy Scouts, the Girl Scouts, Campfire Girls, and so forth; and the various professional organizations, such as the American Medical Association and the American Bar Association. The difference is the same as that indicated in discussing the nurseries. These organizations in the Communist countries are quasi-official and are intended to help inculcate the values of the system. In the United States, these organizations very clearly serve the same purpose, but they do not have a clear official status. Finally, the Communist party member is greatly shaped by his experiences within the party.

The entire educational system is consciously designed to impart the values of the system in addition to providing the individual with the training necessary for him to take his place as a useful member of society. Again, the differences between this type of educational system and the type of educational system that is found in the United States, for example, is that there is a clear-cut, conscious effort to impart the values of the system to the individual. The system in the United States does the same thing, but it is not as clearly organized for that purpose. It would be very difficult to say that the educational system in the United States is not designed to inculcate the values of the system because it is obviously true that the educational system is in fact designed to do this. From the earliest grades we teach the children patriotic little stories about the founding fathers, such as George Washington and the cherry tree, that are intended to present certain values to the child and at the same time present a good image of the American government. The fact that these stories are undoubtedly untrue and are therefore, in this particular example, directly opposed to what the story is trying to teach does not seem to bother anybody.

We teach other stories, such as the story about "the little train that could." We tell the children in essence that, if they try hard enough, they can do anything. We all know, of course, that this is not quite true, but we tell the story to children anyway. Another example is the story of the little train that left the tracks and got into all sorts of trouble. When he got back onto the tracks, he was happy, contented, and accepted. There are so many things that the story is teaching that it is hard to sort them out, but it is obviously suggesting that conformity is good. It is also obviously indicating that acceptance by the group is a goal to be strived for, which is, of course, just another way of looking at the conformity question.[13] Therefore, we do, in the American educational system, from the very beginning, teach children values that we hope they will hold when they grow up. Therefore, our educational system is doing exactly the same thing as the educational system in the Soviet Union or any other country for that matter. This is one of the things that any educational system is designed to do. The values that are taught do vary considerably from country to country, and, of course, one of the purposes of this book is to look at those values that are taught in various countries.

Another key difference between the various approaches to the socialization process in various countries is the degree to which there is a conscious attempt to direct the values of the future generations. We know that in the Soviet Union and in China there is a very clear, very thoroughgoing attempt to do this. We know that in countries such as the United States and England there is also an attempt to do this, but it is not as clearly defined or as consciously recognized, and, because of this, it is impossible for there to be a truly concerted effort to direct values. And the lack of such a concerted effort plus the essentially pluralistic character of the country means that there will be nowhere near the same degree of success or even of effort in directing values in these countries.

One final segment of the social system remains to be mentioned, the social stratification system. There is considerable misunderstanding of what Marxism and Communism have to say regarding social stratification. Engels said that ". . . the proletarian demand for equality is the demand for *abolition of classes*. Any demand for equality which goes beyond that,

---

[13] For a discussion of this type of story, see David Riesman, *The Lonely Crowd: A Study of the Changing American Character* (Garden City, N.Y.: Doubleday Anchor Books, 1953), pp. 128–31.

of necessity passes into absurdity."[14] Thus, Marxism did not argue for the complete elimination of stratification. And Communism has certainly not eliminated it. Both stratification and mobility seem to depend on two factors, membership in the party and education, particularly scientific and technical education. At the same time, an effort is made to achieve some degree of social equality. Concerts, the theater, and all cultural and recreational facilities are made equally available to all, and in this way some of the edge is taken off the stratification system.

Contemporary communism

Although we have actually been discussing contemporary communism for quite some time, there are two characteristics of contemporary communism that require separate consideration, the influence of the discovery of Marx's early writings and the influence of nationalism. We shall take the latter point first because its importance is more firmly established. There are also some other more minor points that will be discussed briefly.

Marx had believed that ultimately the world would all become Communist, both because this was the best system and because the dialectic said so. In assuming a worldwide communism, Marx had thought that class similarities would overcome national differences. This has not proven to be the case. From the very beginning, Communist parties in different countries argued that the revolution in their country would take place slower or faster than in other countries because of national differences. Even Marx had made this point, arguing that certain countries were ripe for revolution while others were not. Stalin also spoke of the development of "socialism in one country," meaning the U.S.S.R., and clearly expressed strongly nationalistic feelings. But this issue was not considered to be important because no one thought that the proletariat would put national sentiment before class sentiment. The fact that they did was seen in World War I and even before, since the proletariat flocked to the cause of the nation against the advice of Communist leaders.

The contemporary influence of nationalism on communism was begun by Marshal Tito of Yugoslavia, who early refused to follow the dictates of the Soviet Union under Stalin, the self-styled and, for a long time, the

---

[14] Engels, *Anti-Dühring*, pp. 147–48. Emphasis in the original.

actual spokesman for communism as a whole. Since Stalin died in 1953, every Eastern European country has loosened, or cut altogether, the ties that bound them to the U.S.S.R. With the exception of Albania, the Eastern European countries have maintained ties with the Soviet Union, but the ties are increasingly loose and probably will never be as tightly tied again. Albania has formed a coalition of sorts with China.

The reasons for these changes are complex, and we do not as yet have sufficient data for valid generalizations, but it seems clear that one of the more important reasons is nationalism. The peoples of these countries, while mostly viewing themselves as Communists, identify more closely with their nation than with communism or the Soviet Union. Each country has a distinct, individual history and culture that the people believe should not be submerged by communism.[15]

A second aspect of contemporary communism which has already been mentioned—the split over the importance of revolution—reflects nationalism. This split is most significant when viewed as part of the basic cleavage of communism into two camps, one led by the Soviet Union, which is fairly moderate, and one led by China, which is militant. Communist parties in most countries of the world seem to have divided along the same lines, one faction supporting coexistence, the other opposing it. Coexistence with non-Communist countries has been the key to this difference. The moderates argue that coexistence is possible or even, because of the bomb held by both sides, essential. Coexistence refers, according to Khrushchev,[16] to the different systems of government. It does not refer to different ideologies because communism is capable of demonstrating that it is a better system and hence will win out in the end through conversion or internal revolt by the proletariat—this was the meaning of Khrushchev's famous "We will bury you."[17] The militants contend that this soft line merely puts off the inevitable conflict and is actually giving in to capitalism. This whole split is also part of a general shift away from

---

[15] See Chapter 6, "The Ideologies of the Developing Nations," for further discussion of the effect of nationalism on Marxism.

[16] See Strobe Talbott, ed. and trans., *Khrushchev Remembers* (Boston: Little, Brown & Co., 1970), p. 512.

[17] In his recent memoirs, Khrushchev reiterated this point saying that he meant that the proletariat in the United States would inevitably overthrow or bury the bourgeois. Ibid., p. 512.

radicalism on the part of successful revolutionary movements, but this topic is beyond the scope of this book.

The third aspect of contemporary communism relates to the problem of leadership change, which is a particularly difficult problem for a dictatorial system. No Communist country has as yet developed a means of smoothly changing from one leader or dictator to the next. Thus, there is a constant struggle for power among the major potential dictators within each Communist country. This struggle for power has a tremendous influence on the way the system operates. It is impossible for any leader to be completely sure of the loyalty of his followers, and particularly, as the leader gets old, there is a jockeying for position among his followers to see who takes over when he dies. Hence, although it may seem that there is a high degree of unity, beneath the surface there is a constant turmoil. This has been clearly seen in the Soviet Union with the ouster of Khrushchev and the sparring among potential leaders since that ouster. Contemporary communism in the period of the dictatorship of the proletariat has failed to provide the smooth transition that Marx had envisioned and has instead produced a system that seems to be incapable of smooth change.

Probably the major current trend in communism is the somewhat belated result of the discovery of Marx's early writings, particularly his *Economic and Philosophic Manuscripts of 1844* (first complete publication was in 1932). The effect of these manuscripts and Marx's other early writings has only been felt in the last ten years or so. This is why they are being discussed here rather than at the beginning of the chapter.

The early Marx was a humanist. He was primarily concerned with the real problems of real people. He pointed to the ways in which people were dehumanized and alienated by the industrial system. Man became the extension of the machine and was further dehumanized by the need to constantly work to earn a living to support himself and his family at even a subsistence level. He was alienated from himself, his fellows, including his own family, and his work.[18] He could not relate well to any other person, he could not find a way to express himself through his work, and he was even cut off from himself. Marx saw the capitalist and industrial systems as the cause; he saw communism as the solution.

---

[18] See Karl Marx, *The Economic and Philosophic Manuscripts of 1844* (Moscow: Foreign Languages Publishing House, 1932).

The new Marxists of Eastern Europe see that some of these problems have not been solved by the introduction of socialism, at least not as it now exists. Therefore, they are returning to this early Marx for inspiration in attacking the real, human problems that exist today, under socialism. They find that Marx's concern with the day-to-day problems of real people help them to criticize the current scene, and they hope thereby to reform socialism as it now functions.

At the same time they have been reading the existentialists, such as Jean-Paul Sartre and Albert Camus. The most obvious link between the early Marx and the atheist existentialists such as Camus and Sartre is found in the idea of alienation. Most of the writings of the existentialists depict modern man cut off from or alienated from nature (Sartre's novel *Nausea* although meaning something very different by nature than did Marx), himself (Camus' play *Caligula*), or the rest of mankind (almost all Camus' writings, particularly the novels *The Stranger* and *The Fall*).

The concerns of the young Marx and the contemporary existentialists are the same and even some of the terms are similar but there are important differences.[19] For our purposes, however, it is more important to note the meeting of the concerns of the young Marx and the contemporary existentialists in the writings of Eastern European Marxists such as Adam Schaff[20] and Lezek Kolakowski.[21] In these writers and a growing number of younger thinkers, one finds the early humanist Marx resurrected. They argue that Marxism must reject many of its own dogmas and return to a concern for the individual human being. They still accept communism; they still reject capitalism. They still argue that capitalism systematically degrades man and that only a system of communism is capable of achieving a society that will truly free man.

It can be seen that they are not rejecting the general lines of their heri-

---

[19] Since we are primarily concerned with contemporary communism, a detailed analysis of these similarities and differences is inappropriate here. The interested reader should consult Raymond Aron, *Marxism and the Existentialists* (New York: Simon and Schuster, 1969); Wilfrid Desan, *The Marxism of Jean-Paul Sartre* (Garden City, N.Y.: Doubleday Anchor Books, 1966); and Walter Odajnyk, *Marxism and Existentialism* (Garden City, N.Y.: Doubleday Anchor Books, 1965).

[20] See, for example, his *Marxism and the Human Individual*, ed., Robert S. Cohen, trans., Olgierd Wojtasiewicz (New York: McGraw-Hill Book Co., 1970).

[21] See, for example, his *Toward a Marxist Humanism; Essays on the Left Today*, trans., Jane Zielonko Peel (New York: Grove Press, 1968).

tage, but are trying to rebuild a new version of Marx's original vision. They are saying that communism must give more scope to the individual; that it must recognize that the goal has not yet been fully realized; that the goal must be explored further; and that short term reform now is highly desirable.

Full communism

The changes in contemporary communism brought about by the fusion of nationalism, the early writings of Marx, and existentialism has given rise to a resurgence of utopian thinking by Marxists. But they have not significantly changed the characteristics of Marx's ideal system, Full Communism. Full Communism has the following characteristics:

1. Distribution of income according to need, no longer according to labor performed.
2. No classes.
3. The state withers away.
4. Very high productivity, so that there is plenty for all.
5. High socialist consciousness—people work without incentives.
6. More equality but not absolute equality.
7. No money.
8. A command economy.
9. The economy managed by a free and equal association of producers.
10. The differences between occupations disappear, so that there is no social distinction between town and country.
11. Each person does about as much physical as intellectual labor.[22]

Full Communism is the goal of the entire system, the utopia toward which all else is aimed. Its general characteristics are not much different from the utopias created by a variety of other socialists throughout the centuries, but some of these characteristics are worth further mention.

The economic aspects of Full Communism are outlined above, and the major similarities and differences between it and the dictatorship of the proletariat are illustrated. The command economy still exists, but it is no

---

[22] Adapted slightly and reprinted by permission of the author and the publishers from P. J. D. Wiles, *The Political Economy of Communism* (Cambridge, Mass.: Harvard University Press, copyright, 1962, by Basil Blackwell & Mott Ltd.), pp. 332–33.

longer controlled by the state. Marx was primarily concerned with abolishing exploitation, and in Full Communism there are no exploiters, only workers. With the exploiters totally gone and the people working without incentives, there should be plenty so that all can be rewarded according to need. The actual organization of the economic system poses a number of problems that will be discussed later.

When turning to other aspects of the society, it is obvious that the most direct effect of a change to Full Communism would be on the social stratification and mobility systems. Since classes would no longer exist and since no distinction would be made between types of labor, there should be no effective social stratification system and thus no social mobility. In the classless or single-class society, there would be no basis for any significant distinctions among man. "Significant" for Marx meant economic, and it would be foolish to assume that he foresaw a complete leveling of men. Individual differences would remain, but they would no longer be distinctions that were detrimental to the individual or the society as they had been under capitalism and all the other socioeconomic systems that preceded it. Occupational mobility would be increased greatly, since an individual would be able to move freely among those positions that interested him. Therefore, social stratification and mobility would become almost meaningless under Full Communism.

Marx envisioned other significant changes in the social system. There would, of course, be no religious system. All crime would disappear because there would be no reason to react against society. In addition, he believed that with the coming of Full Communism prostitution and adultery would disappear and the monogamous family would become a reality. The new family would be based on a love-sex relationship that Marx believed could only have one focus. At the same time, he desired to free women to work. Full Communism would also provide education for all.

With the coming of the classless society, the state would no longer be necessary and would disappear. But it would be replaced by "the administration of things," which means that the economic system would have to be organized and somebody would have to administer it. It would be administered by "a free and equal association of producers," which would have the authority to direct what should be produced and in what amounts, and how it should be distributed. This "free and equal association of producers" could conceivably take a wide variety of forms, depending upon the size of the territory and the complexity of industries within the territory. In attempting to reduce Marx's notion to its fundamentals, most such associations would undoubtedly follow some such pattern as follows. A committee would be selected, probably by election, that would collect data on the productive capacity of the region and the needs of the people. It would then establish priorities and goals for the various manufacturing plants, farms, and craft industries. This all assumes an economy based on abundance and thus would be more concerned with collecting accurate data on needs than establishing priorities. It would be a continuous process, and certainly the composition of the committee would change periodically. Thus, the committee would hold no coercive power, still assuming abundance, and would merely administer the economy.

Full Communism is obviously a utopia. It probably will not, even cannot, ever exist. But it is the goal of Marxism. Many Communists today believe that it will never come. Others believe that it is still possible. But, whichever position one takes, it illustrates some of the appeal that communism has had and will continue to have in the future.

As can now be seen, Marxism and communism are complex, many-faceted ways of viewing the world. Communism as it is today has been treated as the logical extension of Marxism, and in many ways it is, but it must be remembered that we left Marx when we started discussing theories of the revolution and only returned to him with Full Communism. Contemporary communism is as much the product of Lenin, Stalin, Khrushchev, and Mao Tse-tung as it is of Marx, if not more so. The dictatorship of the proletariat was to be a fairly brief period of transition, and for all but a few it has become the final stage. A stage that will change certainly, but it will change internally, gradually being adjusted to the needs and desires of its leaders and the population that they rule rather than consciously driven on to a new stage. But the ideas of Marx have helped greatly to form the thinking of the men who have developed contemporary communism, and Marxism has helped to mold the thinking of those who rule today, and therefore it cannot be neglected. It is difficult to judge precisely the effect that Marx has had on the thinking of these men, but it seems obvious that the world is still viewed through Marx's eyes at least some of the time.

Suggested readings

Marxism

Almond, Gabriel A. *The Appeals of Communism*. Princeton: Princeton University Press, 1954.

Avineri, Shlomo. *The Social and Political Thought of Karl Marx*. Cambridge, Eng.: Cambridge University Press, 1968.

Burns, Emile. *An Introduction to Marxism*. New York: International Publishers Co., 1966.

Cole, G. D. H. *The Meaning of Marxism*. Ann Arbor: University of Michigan Press, 1948.

Curtis, Michael (ed.). *Marxism*. New York: Atherton Press, 1970.

Daniels, Robert V. *The Nature of Communism*. New York: Vintage Books, 1963.

Davis, Horace B. *Nationalism and Socialism; Marxist and Labor Theories of Nationalism to 1917*. New York: Monthly Review Press, 1967.

De George, Richard T. *The New Marxism. Soviet and European Marxism Since 1956*. New York: Pegasus, 1968.

Delfgaauw, Bernard. *The Young Marx*. Trans. Franklin Schutz and Martin Redfern. London: Sheed and Ward, 1967.

Drachkovitch, Milorad M. (ed.). *Marxism in the Modern World*. Stanford, Calif.: Stanford University Press, 1965.

————. (ed.). *Marxist Ideology in the Contemporary World—Its Appeals and Paradoxes*. New York: Frederick A. Praeger, 1966.

Engels, Friedrich. *Selected Writings*. Ed. W. O. Henderson. Baltimore: Penguin Books, 1967.

————. *Socialism: Utopian and Scientific*. Any edition.

Fromm, Erich. *Marx's Concept of Man*. New York: Frederick Ungar Publishing Co., 1966.

———— (ed.). *Socialist Humanism; An International Symposium*. Garden City, N.Y.: Doubleday Anchor Books, 1965.

Gregor, A. James. *A Survey of Marxism; Problems in Philosophy and the Theory of History*. New York: Random House, 1965.

Gyorgy, Andrew (ed.). *Issues of World Communism*. Princeton, N.J.: D. Van Nostrand Co., 1966.

Hunt, R. N. Carew. *The Theory and Practice of Communism; An Introduction*. 5th ed. Baltimore: Penguin Books, 1950.

Jackson, J. Hampden. *Marx, Proudhon and European Socialism*. New York: Collier Books, 1962.

Lenin, V. I. *Imperialism; The Highest Stage of Capitalism.* New York: International Publishers Co., 1939.

———. *State and Revolution.* New York: International Publishers Co., 1943.

———. *What is to be Done?* New York: International Publishers, Co., 1943.

Lichtheim, George. *Marxism; An Historical and Critical Study.* 2nd ed. New York: Frederick A. Praeger, 1965.

Lobkowicz, Nicholas (ed.). *Marx and the Western World.* Notre Dame, Ind.: University of Notre Dame Press, 1967.

Lobriola, Antonio. *Essays on the Materialistic Conception of History.* Trans. Charles H. Kerr. New York: Monthly Review Press, 1966.

Marcuse, Herbert. *Soviet Marxism; A Critical Analysis.* New York: Vintage Books, 1961.

Marx, Karl. *Capital.* Any edition.

———, and Engels, Friedrich. *The Communist Manifesto.* Any edition.

Mayo, Henry B. *Introduction to Marxist Theory.* New York: Oxford University Press, 1960.

Meszaros, Istvan. *Marx's Theory of Alienation.* London: The Merlin Press, 1970.

Meyer, Alfred G. *Communism.* 3rd ed. New York: Random House, 1967.

———. *Leninism.* New York: Frederick A. Praeger, 1957.

———. *Marxism; The Unity of Theory and Practice.* Ann Arbor: University of Michigan Press, 1963.

Petrovic, Gajo. *Marx in the Mid-Twentieth Century; A Yugoslav Philosopher Considers Karl Marx's Writings.* Garden City, N.Y.: Doubleday Anchor Books, 1967.

Sanderson, John. *An Interpretation of the Political Ideas of Marx and Engels.* London: Longmans, Green and Co., 1969.

Schram, Stuart R. *The Political Thought of Mao Tse-tung.* New York: Frederick A. Praeger, 1963.

Seton-Watson, Hugh. *Nationalism and Communism; Essays 1946–1963.* New York: Frederick A. Praeger, 1964.

Tucker, Robert C. *The Marxian Revolutionary Idea.* New York: W. W. Norton & Co., 1969.

———. *Philosophy and Myth in Karl Marx.* Cambridge, Eng.: Cambridge University Press, 1961.

Venable, Vernon. *Human Nature; The Marxian View.* Cleveland, Ohio: World Publishing Co., 1966.

Wetter, Gustav A. *Dialectical Materialism; A Historical and Systematic Survey of Philosophy in the Soviet Union.* Trans. Peter Heath. New York: Frederick A. Praeger, 1958.

The Soviet Union

Armstrong, John A. *Ideology, Politics, and Government in the Soviet Union; An Introduction.* New York: Frederick A. Praeger, 1962.

Bauer, Raymond A., and Inkeles, Alex. *The Soviet Citizen: Daily Life in a Totalitarian Society.* Cambridge, Mass.: Harvard University Press, 1959.

Bauer, Raymond A.; Inkeles, Alex; and Kluckhohn, Clyde. *How the Soviet System Works. Cultural, Psychological and Social Themes.* New York: Vintage Books, 1961.

Berman, Harold J. *Justice in the U.S.S.R.* Rev. ed. New York: Vintage Books, 1963.

Djilas, Milovan. *The New Class. An Analysis of the Communist System.* New York: Frederick A. Praeger, 1957.

Fainsod, Merle. *How Russia Is Ruled.* Cambridge, Mass.: Harvard University Press, 1963.

Kassof, Allen (ed.). *Prospects for Soviet Society.* New York: Published for the Council on Foreign Relations by Frederick A. Praeger, 1968.

Labedz, Leopold (ed.). *International Communism after Khrushchev.* Cambridge, Mass.: M.I.T. Press, 1965.

Osborn, Robert J. *Soviet Social Policies: Welfare, Equality and Community.* Homewood, Ill.: The Dorsey Press, 1970.

Talbott, Strobe (ed. and trans.). *Khrushchev Remembers.* Boston: Little, Brown & Co., 1970.

Wetter, Gustav. *Soviet Ideology Today.* New York: Frederick A. Praeger, 1966.

China

Barnett, A. Doak. *Cadres, Bureaucracy, and Political Power in Communist China.* New York: Columbia University Press, 1967.

――――. *Communist China: The Early Years, 1949–1955.* New York: Frederick A. Praeger, 1964.

Fairbank, John King. *The United States and China.* Rev. ed. New York: Compass Books, 1962.

Geddes, W. R. *Peasant Life in Communist China.* Ithaca, N.Y.: Society for Applied Anthropology, Cornell University, 1963.

Hinton, William. *Fanshen: A Documentary of Revolution in a Chinese Village.* New York: Monthly Review Press, 1967.

Lewis, John Wilson. *Leadership in Communist China.* Ithaca, N.Y.: Cornell University Press, 1963.

———— (ed.). *Major Doctrines of Communist China.* New York: W. W. Norton & Co., 1964.

Liu, William Thomas (ed.). *Chinese Society Under Communism. A Reader.* New York: John Wiley & Sons, 1967.

Myrdal, Jan. *Report from a Chinese Village.* Trans. Maurice Michael. New York: Pantheon Books, 1965.

Snow, Edgar. *The Other Side of the River: Red China Today.* New York: Random House, 1962.

Tsang, Chiu-sam. *Society, Schools and Progress in China.* Oxford, Eng.: Pergamon Press, 1968.

Vogel, Ezra F. *Canton Under Communism: Programs and Politics in a Provincial Capital, 1949–1968.* Cambridge, Mass.: Harvard University Press, 1969.

Yang, C. K. *Chinese Communist Society: The Family and the Village.* Cambridge, Mass.: M.I.T. Press, 1965.

————. *Religion in Chinese Society: A Study of Contemporary Social Functions of Religion and Some of Their Historical Factors.* Berkeley: University of California Press, 1961.

4

DEMOCRACY

Turning from communism to democracy is like finding oneself moved from a lightly wooded hillside with a clear path to the middle of a jungle with no beaten track in sight. With Marxism it was possible to go directly to certain writers and certain key topics without any hesitancy. With democracy there are no specific writers, and there is not even much agreement on what topics must be considered. The amount of literature devoted to statements, analyses, or criticisms of democratic theory is overwhelming, but there is surprisingly little that is at all systematic, and there is even less that discusses the various interrelationships of democracy as a political system with the other aspects of society.

All of this is not too surprising because democracy is not and never has been a clearly defined political theory. There is also no definite way in which democracy as a political system must relate to any other aspect of the social system. This is perhaps most clearly seen in the discussions of the most nearly democratic economic system, which we will look at in some detail later in the chapter.

What we call democracy has evolved over many centuries through modifications both in certain theories that we have called democratic and in the practices of certain countries that have been called democratic. But, at the same time, there has never been a clear definition of what it is that we mean by *democratic*. There are a wide variety of different meanings of the word *democracy*, depending upon the political persuasion of the individual who happens to be speaking at the time. There are those who reject the word as referring more accurately to a state of anarchism. These people usually want to replace the word *democracy* with the word *republicanism* or some such other word, which they feel refers more clearly to a system of government by elected representatives than does the word *democracy*. Others would prefer to see the word *democracy* modified by some other word such as *participatory* to illustrate the need for more activism on the part of the citizenry. With all of these problems in mind, we attempt here to bring some coherence to this mass of data. The reader should be aware that neither the approach used nor certain of the conclusions reached will be acceptable to all, and that other approaches and perhaps other conclusions could have equal, although hopefully not more, validity.

The principles of democracy

The approach used in the following pages is simply an attempt to build a simple model of the key elements of democracy or at least of those elements normally considered significant. They are:

1. Citizen involvement in political decision making
2. Some degree of equality among citizens
3. Some degree of liberty or freedom granted to or retained by the citizenry
4. A system of representation
5. An electoral system—majority rule

Each of these points will be discussed in detail.

Citizen involvement. The most fundamental characteristic of any democratic system, truly its defining characteristic, is the idea that the citizens should be involved in some way in the making of political decisions—either directly or through representatives of their choosing. There are two primary considerations here—the definition of *citizens* and the degree and technique of involvement or participation. The first problem, the definition of citizen, we will look at in connection with political equality because it is most relevant there. The second problem will be discussed at a number of points since it is currently a key issue of democratic theory. Here let us simply look at the distinctions involved.

1. *Direct democracy*—citizens take part in the actual deliberations and voting on issues, rather as if the entire population of a country were to debate and pass upon all laws.

2. *Representative democracy*—citizens choose other citizens to debate and pass upon laws.

Equality. The notion of equality contains five separate ideas that are used in varying combinations by democratic theorists—political equality, equality before the law, equality of opportunity, economic equality, and social equality. Not all of these ideas are generally thought of in the strict sense of equality, which is sameness in relevant aspects. This definition is, of course, quite complex because of the phrase "in relevant aspects."[1]

Assuming for the moment the existence of some sort of representative system, we can look at the first and simplest part of equality—political equality. This includes two separate points—equality at the ballot box and equality in the ability to be elected to public office. Equality at the ballot box entails the following:

1. Each individual must have reasonably easy access to the place of voting.
2. Each individual must be totally free to cast his vote as he wishes.
3. Each vote must be given exactly the same weight when being counted.

Immediately, we note that these conditions are rarely fulfilled. First, there is the problem of citizenship that we noted earlier. All those who are not citizens and all those below a certain age are not politically equal. In addition, there are other groups that are formally discriminated against such as the mentally ill and certain convicted criminals. At times there have been other things added to this list of legal qualifications for voting such as owning a specified amount of property. Until relatively recently women also have not been allowed to vote in most democracies and are still not allowed to vote in some.

Finally, we must note the informal avenues of inequality. First, and perhaps most obvious, is racial discrimination. Second, economic inequality acts to limit the poorer voter by limiting his ability to participate in the selection of candidates. The wealthier voter can significantly affect the campaign effectiveness of a candidate by supporting the campaign financially. Other limitations on the ability of the voter to affect his desires are less obvious—the difficulty of getting to a polling place affects many older voters, and lack of access to complete information affects the ability of

---

[1] See the discussion in J. Roland Pennock and John W. Chapman, eds., *Nomos IX: Equality* (New York: Atherton Press, 1967), particularly the article "Egalitarianism and the Idea of Equality," by Hugo Adam Bedau.

many voters to actually vote for someone who represents their point of view. There are many more.

Equality in the ability to be elected to public office normally means that everyone who has the vote is also capable of being elected to public office, although there are often higher age qualifications and usually some other specific requirements, such as residing in a specified area, for particular offices. In many countries today, it is also becoming very expensive to run for public office, and hence equality in the ability to be elected to public office is being seriously eroded.

Equality before the law is close to the definition of equality as sameness in relevant aspects because it means that all people will be treated in the same way by the legal system, and it is not hedged about by so many formal definitions of relevant aspects. In practice, though, all legal systems have developed a set of informal relevant aspects that depend on such things as wealth, race, or the type of crime involved. In the United States, a series of recent Supreme Court decisions have attempted to eliminate some of these informal requirements for equality before the law. But it should also be noted that these decisions by the U.S. Supreme Court are under attack by many people who view them not as a help to equality before the law, but as a hindrance to the legal system in dealing with criminals.

The third type of equality is related to the social stratification and mobility systems. It is concerned with the ease with which a person can move among the social classes and is equivalent to equality of opportunity. Equality in this sense means, first, that every individual in society will be able to move up or down within the class or status system depending on his ability and his application of that ability. Second, in referring most specifically to equality of opportunity, it means that no *artificial* barrier will keep any person from achieving what his ability and hard work can gain him. The connection between these two types of equality should be fairly obvious because, if equality of opportunity is denied an individual, he will also be denied the ability to freely move up or down within the class or status system. The obvious problem in the definition of equality of opportunity is the word *artificial*, and it has caused much controversy. Normally *artificial* has been applied to such characteristics of an individual as race or religion that in no way affect an individual's inherent abilities. In a number of ways, this problem is also a problem of liberty, and therefore it will be discussed more completely at the appropriate point, as we discuss liberty.

Equality of opportunity is a peculiarly complex concept because it is tied to the social stratification and mobility systems and therefore will vary greatly from society to society. We tend to think of social status and mobility as fairly easily measurable because we almost always link them to an easily quantifiable object—money. In most Western societies today that measure is a fairly accurate guide to status, except at the level of the traditional aristocracy, and the major means of gaining or losing status. But even in the West it is not quite so simple. For example, college professors have traditionally been poorly paid (and still are) but have had a status somewhat higher than their income would dictate. In a society according status on the basis of some other value, such as education, money would not automatically bring status. Therefore, we must remember that equality of opportunity depends on the value that is accorded status and is a much more complex notion than it appears at first.

The fourth aspect of equality, economic equality, is very bothersome. Almost no political philosopher, with the exception of the American, Edward Bellamy,[2] and the Frenchman, Etienne Cabet,[3] has advocated sameness in this regard, but a thorough discussion of this question cannot ignore this exact definition of economic equality. Strictly speaking, economic equality should mean that every individual within the society should have the same income. I believe that this definition is normally avoided because most advocates of economic equality are not primarily concerned with the economic aspects of equality but with the political and legal questions, and with equality of opportunity. In addition, it might be argued that complete equality of income would not itself be fair to all individuals because different individuals have different needs and a complete leveling of income could not take this into account. If, as Bellamy suggested, the income level were sufficiently high, it would be possible for these differences in need to be considered irrelevant because everyone would have enough no matter what his needs might be. But this really is the only way in which this problem of differential need could be overcome.

---

[2] Edward Bellamy (1850–1898) was best known for his utopian novel *Looking Backward* (1888).

[3] Etienne Cabet (1788–1856) founded a series of utopian communities in the United States that were loosely based on his novel *Voyage en Icarie* (1840).

The more common argument for economic equality is that every individual within a society must be guaranteed some level of economic security. The stress here is on security, not equality, and the degree of security varies tremendously. It is contended that, without security, liberty and the other equalities that are essential to democracy are impossible. We have already noted the informal difference that wealth can make before the law. This is also unquestionably true regarding the ability to be elected to public office. In addition, it can be argued that a certain degree of poverty is an artificial barrier in achieving the requirements of equality of opportunity. The effect on voting equality is somewhat more complicated but might be summarized as follows: It is impossible, below a certain level of poverty, to participate actively in the selection of candidates or to know enough about the candidates or the issues to be able to vote intelligently. Persons below this level are also much more open to bribery or other forms of unethical persuasion regarding the use of their votes.

Thus, it can be readily seen that the argument for a degree of economic security which for sake of convenience we tend to call economic equality is based solidly on arguments in favor of the democratic system. The major contention, the key to the whole argument for economic equality in this sense, is the contention that without some degree of economic security the democratic system cannot operate in a democratic manner. It is clear that economic inequality does have an effect on the operation of the democratic system. The problem is whether the effect is great enough to change the system from democracy to something else. Most people today will argue that a too great inequality of income will do this. The questions that are then raised concern, first, how great an inequality is permissible and, second, by what means do you bring the extremes closer together. We shall look at these problems in greater detail as we discuss the differences between democratic capitalism and democratic socialism.

We are discovering that extreme levels of poverty effectively bar an individual from participation in the life of the community. It is impossible to tell to what extent this problem can be solved for those people who have been brought up in what is now known as the culture of poverty, because there seems to be a cumulative effect over a number of generations which makes it more and more difficult for the individual to get out of poverty. This effect is peculiarly significant in education. It has been found that a child in a typical middle-class home or even lower middle-class home has had around him toys and other objects that help to teach him certain of the skills that are essential if he is going to be able to learn easily. A simple thing such as having a book read to him a number of times shows to the child the turning of the pages of the book and normally will show him that the English language is read from left to right and will thus tend to set up a pattern which his eyes will follow.

The child who has not had any of this will start out a year or two or even three behind the more fortunate child. There are also certain skills that a child learns in playing with certain types of toys that are essential even for the relatively unskilled jobs that the poverty-stricken child may be capable of undertaking. A child fitting together pieces of a puzzle or parts of a toy is learning skills that the other child will have to struggle to learn later in school. It has been found that a child from the poverty areas may not even have seen himself in a mirror and may thus have no self-identity, having no idea what he as an individual looks like. The effect of this sort of thing on a child's life can be profound, and we are unsure as to whether some of these effects can be reversed for the child who is already in our school systems. Thus, a child at five or six may already be in a position that he will never be able to get out of. He may already have been lost as a valuable member of society. There are exceptions. There are children who are brought up after generations in this sort of poverty who do make it, but we must be clear that they are the exception, that the overwhelming majority do not make it and in all probability cannot make it because they have simply been left so far behind by the children of parents who can afford simple toys and books and the time to spend with their children.

The fifth type of equality, social equality, is in some ways the most difficult to define because no one seems to be quite clear about what it means. In a narrow sense, perhaps, it can be said that social equality means that no public or private association may erect artificial barriers to activity within the association. Again, there is the problem of defining *artificial*, but generally it would be used in about the same sense as before. Examples of this type of equality might be the lack of artificial barriers to membership in a country club or in use of a public park. A broader notion of social equality can be seen in this description of a hotel in the Soviet Union by the English novelist and poet, Alan Sillitoe. "There was an agreeable classless atmosphere about it. People were either well-dressed, or in quite ordinary clothes, without ties. Workers, scientists, or civil servants —it was impossible to tell which was which. . . ."[4] Sillitoe is making the point that he was impressed, pleasantly impressed, with the degree to which individuals in this hotel could accept one another even though the outward signs of social status or social class were significantly different. These things simply were not important to the people enjoying themselves in this hotel.

Social equality is a fairly intangible thing. It means that a wide variety of people with different backgrounds and different positions and different incomes can get together and all be accepted as if there were no differences. Again, we raise the problem of what are artificial and what might be meaningful barriers to this type of equality. In just discussing poverty, we perhaps came across what becomes a meaningful barrier even though it might have started as an artificial one. An individual from the culture of poverty and an individual from the middle class or lower middle class would have a very difficult time associating with each other because they truly do come from radically different cultures. But this is really an artificial barrier. Complete social equality would mean that the gap could be bridged, that the cultural differences could be overcome and made unimportant. On a simple level, it would mean that the symbols of relative affluence of the middle class would not be essential badges for admission to cultural events, symphonies, and so on, or to restaurants, to places where people go to enjoy themselves. This does not mean that the cultural gap is bridged; it simply means that certain symbols are recognized as unimportant. It means that the poverty stricken, the culturally deprived, are given the opportunity to experience the other culture. Of course, it is likely that poverty will have made it impossible for them even to want to experience the other culture. But social equality would mean that, if somehow they desired to do so, they would be able to.

Liberty. Historically, the desire for equality has often been expressed as an aspect of liberty. When Thomas Jefferson, drafting the Declaration of Independence, spoke of man's equality, he meant that men were equal in the rights they had. Equality of opportunity is often thought of as a right. Thus, there are many ways in which liberty and equality are closely connected in democratic theory. But, in order to understand more

---

[4] Alan Sillitoe, *Road to Volgograd* (London: Pan Books, 1966), p. 46.

fully the ramifications of this curious interrelationship, it is necessary to examine the idea of liberty much more closely.

Liberty, freedom, and right are often used interchangeably. Although some scholars prefer to make careful distinction among the meanings of the three words, it is not necessary to do so. But, whatever term is used, the basic concept is difficult to grasp. All three terms refer to the ability to act either without restriction or to act with restriction but with specified or at least specifiable limits. Freedom means that, in relationship to certain actions, one can act as he wishes without identifiable limits. To say that one has the right to do something means essentially the same thing—no limit should be put on his freedom to act within specified conditions.

There probably is no such thing as complete freedom. In the first place, one must maintain life and perform a number of essential bodily functions. Within limits it is possible to choose the times at which one eats, drinks, sleeps, and so on, but one cannot ignore them altogether. In the second place, there are other people. Although they are essential for a complete life, they do restrict one. There is an old adage that "Your freedom to swing your arm stops at my nose." Although it is superficial, it does point out that the existence of others must be taken into account and thus they do restrict one. Therefore, there is no realistic notion of absolute liberty that can be used as a yardstick against which to measure the limitations one encounters.

Probably the most influential approach to liberty can be found in the distinctions between the rights that man has or should have simply because he is a human being and the rights derived from government. The former are often called natural rights; the latter are called civil rights. Although the trend today is either to reject the concept of natural rights altogether and call all rights civil rights or to replace the word natural with human,[5] it is still instructive to look at the traditional distinction.

Many democratic theorists, such as John Locke,[6] argued that man as man, separate from all government or society, had certain rights which should never be given up or taken away.[7] Man, they argued, could never

---

[5] This change will be discussed more in Chapter 7, "The New Left."

[6] John Locke (1632–1704), author of Two Treatises of Civil Government, which was widely acclaimed by the authors of the American Constitution.

[7] Here I have used the form of argument employed by the so-called social contract theorists because they had a great influence on the development of the notion of liberty in Western thought. See J. W. Gough, The Social Contract; A Critical Study of Its Development, 2nd ed. (Oxford: Clarendon Press, 1957).

give up these rights upon joining a society or government, and the society or government should not attempt to take these rights away; if a government did try to take them away, the people were perfectly justified in revolting to change the government, although not all argued for this last point. The actual content of these natural rights is somewhat more complicated because theorists differed greatly. In all cases the primary consideration was the right to life, and this has had far-reaching implications. The right to life can be interpreted to mean that every person has a right to the necessary minimum of food, clothing, and shelter that is required to live in a given society. Since standards vary considerably from society to society, the necessary minimum might vary a great deal. From this perspective the right to life might include such things as the right to an education equal to one's ability and the right to a job. Normally, the right to life is not developed this fully, but these examples illustrate the complexity of such generalizations. Other natural rights, such as those to happiness or property, have been widely debated but have remained unclarified.

Although there was widespread disagreement on the specific natural rights, it was generally agreed that after the formation of government, these rights must become civil rights or rights that were specifically guaranteed and protected by the government even, or perhaps particularly, against itself. This formulation of liberty obviously raises many problems. Probably the most basic difficulty is found in the assumption that a government will be willing to guarantee rights against itself, but it should be noted that many thinkers have assumed that a representative democracy with fairly frequent elections would solve the problem. Any such government should recognize that an infringement on man's civil rights would insure its defeat in the next election. Experience has shown that this is not necessarily true, and the result has been apathy, civil disobedience,[8] and revolution.[9] At the same time, the protection of liberties is still considered to be one of the primary duties of a democratic political system and an important part of democratic theory.

---

[8] See, for example, Robert A. Goldwin, ed., *On Civil Disobedience; American Essays Old and New* (Chicago: Rand McNally & Co., 1969); and Howard Zinn, *Disobedience and Democracy; Nine Fallacies on Law and Order* (New York: Vintage Books, 1968).

[9] See, for example, Franz Marek, *Philosophy of World Revolution; A Contribution to an Anthology of Theories of Revolution,* trans., Daphne Simon (New York: International Publishers, 1969); Truman Nelson, *The Right of Revolution* (Boston: Beacon Press, 1968); and Abdul A. Said and Daniel M. Collier, *Revolutionism* (Boston: Allyn and Bacon, 1971).

It is somewhat more difficult to describe types of liberty than it was to discuss types of equality but, loosely, civil rights seem to generally include the following specific liberties or freedoms:

Right to vote
Freedom of speech
Freedom of the press
Freedom from arbitrary treatment by the political and legal system
Freedom of religion
Freedom of movement
Freedom of assembly

In addition, there are other freedoms that vary according to the particular type of economic system that is combined with the democratic political system. These aspects of liberty will be considered in more detail later.

Another important aspect of liberty is found in the fact that there is no peculiarly democratic social organization except in the very loose sense that a democratic society should be fairly free and open rather than controlled. It is the general assumption of democratic theory that whatever does no damage to the society as a whole or to the individuals within it should be the concern of no one but the individual or individuals involved.

This means that there is no peculiarly democratic family organization. It further means a broad tolerance for varying belief systems. This tolerance of diverse belief systems tends toward the separation of church and state and to freedom of inquiry within the educational system. This also should lead to the freedom of the mass media to publish or broadcast without censorship. It will be clear to anyone minimally aware of the state of the world today that no democracy actually achieves these ideals.

Finally, the social stratification and social mobility systems must be flexible and open to anyone depending solely on ability and hard work. It should be clear that no democratic system in the world has actually achieved this broad tolerance of diversity within the social system. It should also be clear that tolerance means simply the acceptance of this diversity, not the approval of it. Therefore, tolerance is merely one stage in a continuum of attitudes toward diversity. Tolerance varies considerably from country to country. Comparative research has shown a wide diversity in such probable indicators of tolerance as freedom of press, freedom of speech, and so forth. All these systems, but particularly the social stratification and social mobility systems, are strongly influenced by the peculiarities of the economic systems.

Each of these liberties is limited to some extent by all political systems including democratic ones. The democratic system has built into it certain safeguards that are supposed to protect the individual from having his freedoms too severely restricted. Of course they do not always work. The most fundamental of these safeguards is the basic characteristic of a democracy—the people have some control over their government. Democratic theorists have never adequately dealt with the problem of severe restrictions of rights when they are desired by or acquiesced in by the majority. In modern representative democracies, this problem is made more complex because of the various roles assumed by the representatives. Therefore, we will look at the representative system next.

The system of representation. The most obvious problem with direct democracy was that it could only function in a country that was fairly small, both in territory and population.[10] Because of this difficulty, a number of theories of representation developed,[11] and hence sometimes contemporary democracy is known as representative democracy.[12] Theories of representation present virtually as great a difficulty to the understanding as does democracy itself. The greatest difficulty among theories of representation has developed from attempts to view it as a means of achieving a secondhand direct democracy. But there are three senses in which the word *represent* is viewed that help provide an understanding of the problem. First, we often say that something represents something else when it is a faithful reproduction or an exact copy of the original. Second, we use the word *represent* in the sense of an object symbolizing another object. Third, we sometimes use the word *represent* in the sense of a lawyer acting for or in place of his client. These three senses of representation, particularly the differences between the first and the third, contain much of the problem that representation holds for democratic theory. In addition,

---

[10] Most democratic theorists have taken this position, but there is a growing belief that the system could be applied to different conditions. See the section, "Contemporary Trends," later in this chapter.

[11] See Hanna Fenichel Pitkin, *The Concept of Representation* (Berkeley: University of California Press, 1967).

[12] Some who oppose the use of the word *democracy* applied to contemporary political systems base their arguments on this point. They contend that the word *democracy* refers solely to the type of system that existed in ancient Athens in which each individual represented himself rather than electing someone to represent him.

the following selection taken from a famous speech of Edmund Burke to the Electors of Bristol illustrates a further distinction that bothers theorists of representation and practical politicians alike.

To deliver an opinion is the right of all men; that of constituents is a weighty and respectable opinion, which a representative ought always rejoice to hear, and which he ought always most seriously to consider. But *authoritative* instructions, *mandates* issued, which the member is bound blindly and implicitly to obey, to vote, and to argue for, though contrary to the dearest conviction of his judgment and conscience,—these are things utterly unknown to the laws of this land, and which arise from a fundamental mistake of the whole order and tenor of our Constitution.

Parliament is not a *congress* of ambassadors from different and hostile interests, which each must maintain, as an agent and advocate, against other agents and advocates; but Parliament is a *deliberative* assembly of *one* nation, with one interest, that of the whole where not local purposes, not local prejudices, ought to guide, but the general good, resulting from the general reason of the whole. You choose a member, indeed; but when you have chosen him, he is not a member of Bristol, but he is a member of *Parliament*. If the local constituent should form a hasty opinion evidently opposite to the real good of the rest of the community, the member for that place ought to be as far as any other from an endeavor to give it effect.[13]

Here Burke presents a case for the representative as an indepedent agent who represents something solely in the sense that he is elected by the people in a particular area. In doing this, he specifically rejects representation in the sense of our third definition of agent for some individual or group.

Thus, we are presented with four differing definitions of representation, all of which have played and still do play important roles in the various theories and systems of representation that have influenced the structure and operation of democratic government. A fifth theory might be added that is composed of elements of all but Burke's position. It is sometimes argued that the representative should be a microcosm of the multiplicity of interests that are found in his constituency with each interest being part of him to the exact extent that it is important within his district. It is highly unlikely that this is possible, but some representatives try to achieve it. Seldom, if ever, will it be true that an elected official will exactly fit one and only one of the roles assigned by these theories of representa-

---

[13] Speech to the Electors of Bristol (1774) in *The Works of the Right Honorable Edmund Burke*, 7th ed. (Boston: Little, Brown & Co., 1881), vol. II, p. 96. Emphasis in the original.

tion. Even the most Burkean of representatives will have to act as an agent for his constituency at times or on certain issues if he expects to be elected.[14] The typical representative is likely to act as an agent for his constituents whenever they are directly concerned with a particular issue with which he has to deal. He is also likely to act as an agent in assisting individuals or groups of his constituents when they are dealing with the bureaucracy and feel the need of some assistance. At the same time, the typical representative is likely to act as the Burkean representative on issues that do not directly concern or interest his constituency and thus on which he receives little or no pressure from his constituency. In addition, he may at times ignore pressure from his constituency and act in what he believes to be the best interest of the nation as a whole. Again, he would be acting as a Burkean representative.

One of the key issues within representative democracy is the concern of some theorists to equate representative and direct democracy. In the U.S. system such practices as the initiative,[15] referendum,[16] and recall[17] were developed as devices to allow the people as a whole to play a direct role in political decision making. This problem can perhaps be seen most clearly in the thinking of Jean Jacques Rousseau.[18] At one point he says, "Thus deputies of the people are not, and cannot be, its representatives; they are merely its agents, and can make no final decisions. Any law which the people have not ratified in person is null, it is not a law."[19] Here Rousseau has used two of our definitions of *represent*. For him *represent* cannot refer to an agent but must refer to an exact copy but, since the latter is impossible among men, he rejects the idea of representative democracy. Still, Rousseau realized that within a large country direct democracy was impractical, and even impossible, and, although he main-

---

[14] See the discussion of roles played by United States senators in this regard and others in Donald R. Matthews, *U.S. Senators and Their World* (New York: Vintage Books, 1960), pp. 218–42.

[15] Initiative—a method by which a new law may be proposed directly by the voters by means of a petition.

[16] Referendum—a method by which the voters may pass on legislation already passed by a legislative body.

[17] Recall—a method by which an official may be removed from office during his term by a vote of the people.

[18] Jean Jacques Rousseau (1712–78), famous French political philosopher best known for his book *De Contrat social (The Social Contract)*.

[19] Jean Jacques Rousseau, *De Contrat social* (Paris: La Renaissance du Livre, n.d.), p. 86.

tains the ideal of direct democracy, he does discuss representation in a more favorable light. He says:

I have just shown that government weakens as the number of magistrates [read elected officials] increases; and I have already shown that the more numerous the people is, the more repressive force is needed. From which it follows that the ratio of magistrates to government should be in inverse proportion to the ratio of subjects to sovereign; which means that the more the state expands, the more the government ought to contract; and thus that the number of rulers should diminish in proportion to the increases of the population.[20]

If possible Rousseau would like to see a country small enough so that every man could be his own representative, but as population rises this becomes more and more difficult, and thus the number of rulers must of necessity diminish through the establishment of some type of representative system. But he strongly believes that, the closer that a system can come to a direct democracy through an increase in the number of magistrates, the better the system will be.[21]

Rousseau's approach to representation has regained favor in recent years in the movement known as participatory democracy. Although it will be discussed more thoroughly later,[22] it is appropriate at this point to note that the idea of the people as a whole ratifying the actions of their agents has been a common thread in U.S. political thought exemplified by the initiative, referendum, and recall.

There has also been another thread in U.S. political thought, not as common perhaps, that was more directly along the line of participatory democracy in that it emphasized individual responsibility rather than the responsibility of the people as a whole. The participatory democrat argues that the individual should not be bound by laws that he himself did not in some way help to make or participate in making. In other words the individual, all individuals, must be consulted in the making of laws that are going to affect them. If they are not consulted, the law is considered invalid. The law is also considered invalid if the individual feels that it is unjust. This is an attempt to make the representative more responsive to the wishes of his constituents and, in another sense, to bring the whole

---

[20] Ibid., p. 59.
[21] See Rousseau's discussion of such a system in *Projet de constitution pour la Corse* ("Constitutional Project for Corsica"), in Rousseau, *Political Writings*, trans. and ed., Frederick Watkins (London: Thomas Nelson & Sons, 1953), pp. 277–330.
[22] See Chapter 7, "The New Left."

representative system more in line with the ideas and ideals of direct democracy.

Electoral system. In this discussion of representation, it is important not to lose sight of what is the primary purpose of the representative system in a democracy, that is, to provide a means for the people of the country to exercise some control over political decision making when they cannot directly exercise it themselves. This means that the representative will not automatically be expected to serve for life, and thus some method must be devised so that the people can either maintain him in, or remove him from, office. This brings us to the institution of periodic elections. Many scholars argue that the electoral system is a major defining characteristic of a democracy,[23] particularly the system by which the majority rules. The electoral system is as important an issue in democratic theory as the theory of representation because it is the primary way of insuring some governmental responsiveness to the wishes of the people. In a large, complex society, the vote may be the only way in which the majority of the people ever participate in the control of political decision making.

Because of this limited participation by many citizens, the electoral system takes on a much greater significance for democratic theory than it would otherwise. With a few exceptions the specific institutional arrangements of elections are not of much importance, but the exceptions are noteworthy. The normal rule of elections is clearly that the side with the most votes wins, but this seemingly clear principle of majority rule is in fact fairly complicated. First, it in no way assumes that the $50\% + 1$ of the voters is right and the $50\% - 1$ is wrong. It merely says that since more people voted for A rather than B, A must be temporarily accepted.

Unfortunately, this point is not always recognized; furthermore, this approach tends to assume that any issue has only two sides. If, for example, there are three candidates in any given election, majority rule becomes more complicated since it is harder to clearly determine what the majority wants. Since relatively few potential voters actually cast their ballot in many elections, the majority may also not actually be represented in the result. This objection may, of course, be answered that those who do not vote, do not care, but it might also be answered that their desires were not represented by any side in the election. This difficulty indicates

[23] For example, see Henry B. Mayo, *An Introduction to Democratic Theory* (New York: Oxford University Press, 1960), pp. 72–106.

the advantage of having more than two candidates in an election, but we have already seen the disadvantage of such an arrangement—if no one receives a clear majority, does this constitute majority rule? Thus, at times various governments have made it difficult or even impossible for more than two sides to be represented on the ballot. An additional institutional arrangement that raises serious problems is the common practice in the United States of requiring more than a simple majority on certain issues, particularly on bond issues. This clearly says that the minority should have a veto on certain issues.

Again, we have the whole problem of participation in the political system brought before us, and it should be clear by now that this is one of the major issues of democratic theory. The electoral system, although seemingly merely a mechanism for determining the composition of the government over the next few years, actually provides the major and sometimes the sole means of political participation for individuals living within a large, complex, modern society such as the United States. In such cases the electoral system takes on peculiar importance for democratic theory because, if it does provide the sole means of political participation, or even the major means of political participation for an individual, it is the key to whether the system is democratic or not. An individual, when going into the voting booth, must be sure that his vote will be counted, and we assume that he is voting in an election where he is provided with some choice, and we assume that the choice is meaningful in the sense that he is actually free to vote for any of the options that are provided. It is also important to remember the most obvious point, that is, he is allowed to vote in the first place.

Finally, each individual's vote should be equal to any other individual's vote. This last point is disputed by some who believe themselves to be democratic and who argue that there are individuals who are worth more to the community than the normal run-of-the-mill citizen and that these individuals should be provided with more votes on the basis of some formula such as the amount of taxes paid. This argument is not a common one by any means, but it illustrates an important point. It shows that there are fundamental disagreements over all aspects of the electoral system. Not everyone is allowed to vote within any country. There are commonly elections in every country in which there is only one candidate, and as we have seen there are those who contend that not all votes should be counted equally.

The problems deriving from the specific arrangements of the electoral system and the principle of majority rule are not themselves of prime importance, but these questions of electoral procedure imply other, more important problems. The electoral system itself, in addition to providing a means of political participation, is significant in providing the means for the peaceful change of political power from one individual or group to another. This in turn raises the whole problem of leadership within a democracy, a question that has bothered democratic theorists since ancient Athens.[24] The importance of leadership in democratic theory cannot be gainsaid, and in representative democracy it is peculiarly significant. Whatever theory of representation is accepted, the elected official is given some political power that is not directly held by his constituents. This power can be removed through the electoral process but, in the meantime, it is held by an individual who can thus directly participate in political decision making to the extent of the power invested in his office. In addition, he may also exercise political leadership in the sense that he can help to form or inform the opinions of his constituency and others by defining the political issues that he believes to be significant and by propagandizing for particular points of view or positions.[25]

Historically, most democratic theorists have been concerned with attempting to limit the political power held by any one individual or group within the society while at the same time providing intelligent and capable leadership. For example, James Madison, an important figure in the framing of the U.S. Constitution, was greatly worried about the possibility of some faction, including a "majority faction," gaining political power and

---

[24] On this problem see Peter Bachrach, *The Theory of Democratic Elitism: A Critique* (Boston: Little, Brown & Co., 1967); Henry K. Girvetz, *Democracy and Elitism: Two Essays with Selected Readings* (New York: Charles Scribner's Sons, 1967); Dennis F. Thompson, *The Democratic Citizen; Social Science and Democratic Theory in the Twentieth Century* (New York: Cambridge University Press, 1970); and Carole Pateman, *Participation and Democratic Theory* (New York: Cambridge University Press, 1970).

[25] The complexity of the role of leadership in public opinion formation is such that it cannot be discussed here in any detail. The following items will provide the reader with an introduction to this field: See, for example, Robert E. Lane and David O. Sears, *Public Opinion* (Englewood Cliffs, N.J.: Prentice-Hall, 1963). For a more intensive analysis see V. O. Key, Jr., *Public Opinion and American Democracy* (New York: Alfred A. Knopf, 1961). The best current survey of the literature is Edward C. Dreyer and Walter A. Rosenbaum, eds., *Public Opinion and Behavior; Essays and Studies*, 2nd ed. (Belmont, Calif.: Wadsworth Publishing Co., 1970).

exercising it in their own interest. Thus, Madison and most of the other writers of the American Constitution advocated an enlightened leadership of aristocracy exercising political power but periodically checked through election, rather than rule by the people, even indirectly. In other words, they accepted Burke's theory of representation and made it the essence of their theory of government.

Democracy and the economic system[26]

Probably the most controversial topic among those who consider themselves to be democrats is the economic system that is most democratic—capitalism or socialism. In the next few pages we will look at each contender, not with a view to permanently settling the issue, but simply with the intention of understanding what the debate is all about.

Democracy and capitalism. Capitalism is an economic system that has changed greatly over the years. Traditionally, capitalism meant a system characterized by:

1. Private ownership of property
2. No limitation on the accumulation of property
3. The absence of governmental intervention in the economy

Today capitalism is characterized by:

1. Most property held privately
2. Little actual limit on the accumulation of property
3. Governmental *regulation* of the economy
4. A growing welfare system

The distinctions between these two systems must be kept in mind because many discussions of capitalism confuse the picture by mixing the two systems. Traditional capitalism is not accepted by many people today, but too many people do talk about capitalism as if it were still the traditional system.

Capitalists of both persuasions see the major democratic aspect of capitalism in liberty, but they approach it differently. For example, the defenders of traditional capitalism contend that the whole edifice of liberty is founded upon private property and would be destroyed if the amount of property that can be held by any one individual were limited. Since

---

[26] It is impossible to do more than introduce this large topic. For further material see the suggested readings at the end of the chapter.

government is the only organization powerful enough to limit property holding, this question immediately shifts to the problem of governmental intervention in the economy. The modern capitalist argues along slightly different lines. He might say that, admittedly a limit on property would infringe liberty and would change the traditional system, but that some sort of limit can be put on the amount held by any given individual. This would then enable more people to hold property and hence would provide for a wide-based liberty.

Modern capitalists also argue that, the more widespread property holding is within the system, the more viable capitalism is. Property holding, they contend, helps to overcome the problems of poverty that affect all economic systems today. The amount of property and the amount of money that individuals hold directly affects the amount of money that they spend. The amount of money that they spend directly affects the amount that any industry in a country can produce; the amount that they produce obviously affects the number of people that they can hire; the number of people they can hire again affects the amount of money that is in the system, and thus can be spent for the products of the company; the amount of products that the company can produce obviously then affects the profit of the company. In this way, it is argued that some limitation on the amount of property or money that can be held by any individual can in fact help the entire capitalist system rather than be a detriment to it.

This first argument is not as important as the one centering more specifically on governmental intervention in the economy, particularly in the sense of governmental regulation of the economy. The argument of traditional capitalists would not change. Any governmental intervention in the economy, they contend, would destroy the basis for the capitalist system; hence, individualism and liberty. But the defenders of some governmental regulation, although admitting that it must not entail control of the economy, say that the complete absence of governmental regulation acts itself to destroy the democratic capitalist system because a very few people would be able to control the economy and even the government through the establishment of monopolies.[27]

This was certainly the case in the United States in the period of the great expansion of the railroads and of industrialism in general. Such men as J. P. Morgan, J. J. Hill, and the Rockefellers virtually controlled the

---

[27] There are many other bad effects of a lack of governmental regulation, but the development of monopolies is the most important politically.

American economy and by doing so the American government. This monopolistic tendency, the modern capitalist would argue, destroys the capitalist system by radically limiting the number of companies or individuals who can adequately compete within the system. It is not a capitalist system when a few companies can set the prices on virtually all the goods within a country. Thus, relatively few new men with new ideas or new approaches would be able to experiment with them in the system. It would not be talent that would show in the system, it would be the monopolist's will. This does not fit the image of the capitalist system that presents us so often with the myth of the office boy who becomes corporation president through diligent work. The office boy of a monopolist might become a business president someday, but it would not necessarily be through diligent work. The key factor would be the whim of the monopolist, not the talent of the office boy.

Thus, the monopoly system cannot be seen as the ideal system of capitalism. But it is the system that totally unregulated capitalism became. Probably the most important of these points, viewed from the perspective of democratic theory, is the control of the government that could be exercised by the monopolist. Such control would obviously severely restrict the degree to which democracy could exist because it might even negate the effect of popular participation in political decision making. It will be recalled by some that President Eisenhower, in his farewell address, warned the American people about a military-industrial complex that he contended was close to ruling the United States through informal channels. This is the sort of thing that could happen even more readily under a monopoly system.[28] Thus, although regulation of monopolies is not the only form of governmental intervention in the economy, for our purpose it is the most significant.

Modern capitalism is often called a mixed economy, which indicates that, although most property is held privately, extensive property is publicly owned. It also signifies that the government, the public, is active in the manufacturing and distribution of goods, even though this is also primarily in private hands. The changes in capitalism from the traditional to the mixed system are all changes in degree, not in kind. Private ownership

---

[28] The New Left contends that it has already happened. See Chapter 7 and Paul A. Baran and Paul M. Sweezy, *Monopoly Capital; An Essay on the American Economic and Social Order* (New York: Monthly Review Press, 1966).

is still the major means of property holding; wealth is somewhat limited by the system of taxation, but immense fortunes can still be accumulated. Unquestionably, government does intervene in the economy and intervene extensively, but it acts primarily to ensure that the game is played fairly and to see that the losers will not starve.

Of course, there are many who contend that this is not the manner in which the government in the democratic capitalist system, particularly in the United States, does intervene, but that it intervenes for other reasons, reasons that relate more to the control of the economy than to the regulation of the economy. There are those who also argue that the government does not see that the game is played fairly, but that it supports certain of the players who do not necessarily play fairly through its enormous spending power. At the same time, there are examples of the business community playing unfairly with the government, charging it enormous sums for such inexpensive items as paper clips, for example. In addition, it should be noted that regulation of such an enormous operation as the capitalist system in the United States is virtually impossible. No one can know everything that is going on. No bureaucracy, however large, can keep its fingers on all the possible questionable dealings. The regulation, then, is of necessity somewhat sporadic, but the modern capitalist would argue that even this sporadic regulation helps to avoid the excesses of monopoly.

Capitalism has changed; there can be no question of that, but it still exists and will exist as long as the private sector of the economy is larger than the public. Whether or not it is a good system is not the question here. At this point we are only concerned with description and with the relationship between capitalism and democracy. This relationship can be stated quite simply. Capitalism as an economic system is not directly concerned with participation in political decision making, except as was noted above. On the other hand, capitalism is directly concerned with equality and liberty. Capitalism stresses equality of opportunity and is primarily concerned with economic freedom in the sense that each person is freely and equally able to enter the marketplace and succeed or fail on the basis of his abilities and the consumer's desire and need for his product or service. Capitalism is not directly concerned with, or related to, the other aspects of liberty or equality.

In this light it would seem, at least on the surface, a little foolish to speak of capitalism as a particularly democratic system. Capitalism takes cognizance of only a very limited part of two of the defining characteristics of democracy, and these two parts are solely related to the economic system. Why then do so many people believe that capitalism is the only system that can fit with a democratic political system? There are, of course, many arguments based primarily upon patriotic feelings about the democratic capitalist system that exists in the United States. In essence, many argue that, because the United States has been economically and politically successful, the combination of systems that exists in this country has to be the best.

This sort of argument is questionable at best, and we must look for sounder reasons. The main argument stems from the belief that capitalism allows more freedom for the individual than does any other economic system. This argument is based on the freedom of action within the economic system that is provided in capitalism. Any individual with sufficient interest and sufficient funds can buy stock in any number of companies within a democratic capitalist system. In this way, individuals can become part of the working of the economic system. They become part owners of a company or companies. They can, if they have the time and the money, participate in some decisions of the company at the annual meetings, although it must be noted that this ability is very limited for the small shareholder. It is also possible for any individual with the money and the energy to go into business for himself. If he has a product that people want, he may be successful. If he has a product that people either do not want or cannot afford, he will fail. But the point is not that he succeeds or that he fails, but that the system allows him to make an attempt, even though it may or may not encourage him to make the attempt, depending on the circumstances of the times.

This is the democratic aspect of capitalism. Freedom of the individual to enter the economic system, again, under some governmental regulation, and some limitation due to the existence of many large corporations, and to succeed or fail upon his own willingness to work hard and the desire of the consumer, manipulated to some extent by advertising, to buy his product. It should be noted that this freedom is overwhelmingly an economic freedom. It has very little if anything to do with the political aspects of democracy. And this is one of the main reasons why capitalism is primarily concerned with equality of opportunity among the various equalities that we discussed, because the system says that every man should be able to become a capitalist and have the potential of getting rich. If equality of opportunity does not exist, this is, of course, not true.

Because of this concern with equality of opportunity, the mixed economy has recently begun to develop a welfare system designed to ensure that everyone within the society will actually have an equal opportunity to succeed within the society. This system has tended to develop haphazardly without any overall planning, but it is based on the growing realization that certain levels of poverty make it almost impossible for those at these levels to get the necessary motivation and skills to succeed. This concern is not solely based on humanitarian ends but also on the recognition that such people are in fact a burden on society and a tremendous waste of potential manpower. In addition, welfare programs have been concerned with the aged, who have contributed to society but who need help to provide for their period of retirement when many costs, such as medical bills, tend to rise and their incomes decline. This welfare system has been developed more thoroughly and less haphazardly under democratic socialism because it has been concerned with a broader definition of equality than has democratic capitalism.

Welfare systems around the world are coming under tremendous criticism recently for doing exactly what they were designed to do, for being *welfare* systems, for being systems that give away money rather than providing an individual with the means of earning it himself. This sort of criticism is peculiarly appropriate and peculiarly common in the capitalist system because, in effect it is saying that this system, this welfare system, is not providing the equality of opportunity that capitalism desires. What it is actually doing is removing people from the mainstream of economic life, giving them a subsistence on which to live and not allowing them to enter into the capitalist system even at the most minimal level of wage earner.

Today the system is also being criticized on different grounds by the recipients of the welfare. They have recognized what it does to them, how it keeps them in a state of poverty, not allowing them to get out. The recipients of the welfare system have also been treated poorly by the bureaucracies that have been designed to distribute the funds. Too often these bureaucracies have failed to even attempt to understand the human problems that they are supposedly solving. This is understandable because, of course, these bureaucracies have been tremendously overburdened with work. The people staffing them have been badly paid. There has been little status in the job. And one who lives from day to day with human misery must begin at some point to establish a mechanism so that it does not affect him. They must be, at least to some extent, uninvolved in the cases that come before them or else they might be overcome and perhaps unable to function at all.

For all of these reasons, the welfare system is under heavy attack. It has also never really been adequate to the needs in any country; under democratic capitalism, as we noted, it has developed haphazardly in an unplanned way and thus has been even less able to face the problems that it has encountered. We cannot predict what will replace the welfare system, but it can be said with some certainty that the welfare system will be replaced, that it must be replaced, and that the capitalist system must, perhaps in order to survive, come up with some other way of overcoming the problems of poverty that exist within it, some way of actually insuring the equality of opportunity that is basic to a successful capitalist system. There are, of course, no easy solutions to any of these problems, but solutions must be found. The democratic socialist system, with a much more thoroughly developed welfare system, faces some of the same problems. The advocates of democratic socialism, though, contend that the basic difference in the system, the existence of the socialist system, is a major step toward the solution of some of these problems. Therefore, let us now look briefly at democratic socialism.

Democracy and socialism. The fundamental assumption underlying democratic socialism is that participation in political decision making should be extended to economic decision making. This basic assumption is not always clearly stated, but it is probably the single most important argument put forth by democratic socialists because it most solidly places them within democratic theory, more solidly than democratic capitalism. The democratic socialists argue that, since economy and politics are so closely intertwined, the voter should be in a position to control his economic future through the government he elects. And they also argue that the democratic capitalist system places too much power in the hands of individuals and groups that cannot be checked at the polls and that these individuals and groups must be placed under the direct control of the people through the electoral process.

If one assumes that the people in a country should control their political lives, should have some say at least in the process of political decision making, it is only a very short step to the democratic socialist argument that the people should have some say in economic decision making. There is no question that economic decisions in connection with, for example, a steel industry have tremendous impact on an entire country. Therefore, the democratic socialists argue that there must be some means devised by which the people can have an ultimate check on the economic decisions made that do affect a significant portion of the country. Of course, it is difficult to draw a line. What economic decisions are significant in this sense? What industries are key industries for a national economy? Democratic socialists would argue that these decisions should be made by the elected representatives of the people, and that the decisions are likely to vary from country to country. In addition, the forms of governmental control and regulation are likely to vary from country to country, again, depending upon the decisions made by the elected representatives of the people checked, of course, at the polls by the people themselves.

Another argument for democratic socialism, perhaps the most appealing one, is what one might call the humanitarian argument. Democratic socialists contend that the capitalist system has failed to solve the fundamental problems of poverty, disease, and so forth, that face a country. They say that capitalism is probably capable of solving these problems but, since the economic decision makers are not checked in any way by the needs and desires of people as a whole, they have ignored these basic problems. The democratic socialist argues that only when the economic system is ultimately controlled by the people will solutions to these problems be possible. They say that the capitalist is too concerned with profit, that he must be concerned with the people in the country, but that the capitalist system makes it impossible for any systematic attack to be made on these problems. Therefore, they say that democratic socialism is essential if we are going to overcome the most basic problems of society, since only under democratic socialism can the people demand solutions.

The difference in means, though, is the most obvious distinction between the two systems. Democratic socialism can be loosely characterized as follows:

1. Much property held by the public through the democratically elected government, including all the major industries, utilities, and transportation
2. A limit on the accumulation of private property
3. Governmental regulation of the economy
4. An extensive welfare system

It should be recognized that democratic socialist systems in practice vary considerably from country to country, particularly in the degree to which the industries, utilities, transportation, and so forth, are directly owned by the government. In some countries, all of these are governmentally owned. In other countries, there is a considerable limitation in which only specific parts of industrial complexes are owned by the government. For example, in England not all of the steel industries are governmentally owned—some are in private hands and some are owned by the government. And in England this is the pattern throughout most of the major industries.

When we say that much property is held by the public, this refers to property that is directly relevant to the functioning of the economic system. It does not mean that there is no private property. Private property is still held by the individual in such things as his personal belongings, housing, and most small businesses, and in some cases large corporations are still held privately. The publicly held property is the property that is crucial to the operation of the economic system, such as transportation, steel, mining, and so forth. Some democratic socialists, theorists, and systems do not limit the amount of private property that can be held by an individual but others do. There is no inherent necessity within democratic socialist theory for there to be such limitations. On the other hand, the humanitarian argument for democratic socialism referred to before could lead one to argue that some degree of redistribution of income would be justified and that one way of doing this would be to put a limit on private property.

The government under a democratic socialist system clearly will regulate that part of the economy that it does not own directly. This regulation will be to insure that the businesses that are privately owned are operated in the best interests of the society as a whole, rather than simply for private profit. This point is illustrative of the ethos of democratic socialism as opposed to that of democratic capitalism. Democratic socialism is concerned with society as a whole. The word socialism refers to social theories rather than to theories that are oriented toward the individual, and democratic socialism, placing its stress solidly on the public as the center of political and economic power, more clearly than almost any other socialist theory is a social theory, a theory concerned with the people as a whole rather than with individuals within it. Democratic capitalism is a theory concerned with the individual and only secondarily with society or the public as a whole. This is not to say, of course, that either democratic socialism or democratic capitalism forgets the other side. It simply illustrates where the emphasis of the theory lies.

This emphasis helps to illustrate some of the differences between the two theories. Both are concerned with the individual. Both are concerned with the welfare of all within the society. But democratic socialism places its stress on individual equality and the society as a whole; democratic capitalism stresses the economic individual.

In addition to the democratic proposition proclaimed in the basic assumption noted above, the theory suggests that liberty cannot be maintained without some minimal economic equality. This argument is the same as that of the modern democratic capitalist for the welfare state as a means of securing equality of opportunity, but it is broader in the sense that it is demanding more than equality of opportunity. The democratic socialist says that neither the right to vote nor any other form of liberty is possible unless every person within the society is economically secure. If anyone is economically insecure, he will be incapable of exercising his liberty. This economic security can be ensured only through an extensive welfare system.

This extensive welfare system of democratic socialism has some of the same problems as has the welfare system under democratic capitalism. The major differences are two: first, the extent of the system in which many more things are covered than are covered in the democratic capitalist system; second, the way in which the system is financed. It is supposedly but not always different under democratic capitalism. Of course, the system is financed directly from taxes. In the democratic socialist system, there are often taxes to help finance the system, but profit from the nationalized industries, the industries owned by the government, can also be used to help finance the system. This, of course, does not mitigate the problems of any welfare system, as we noted when talking about democratic capitalism. They still exist and they must be solved.

The typical democratic socialist welfare system includes an extensive medical care system that is either free or is provided at minimal cost. This includes prenatal care for mothers, dental care, and eye examinations, in addition to the more typical health services. There is an obvious practical rationale for an extensive health system in the fact that a healthy individual can contribute more to society than can a sick one. Therefore, it is certainly to the advantage of the society as a whole to insure that everyone within it is healthy. This is, of course, the fundamental rationale of any welfare system—that an individual who is maintained at the minimum level of life can make a contribution to society. The welfare system is also designed to take care of those who have already made a contribution to society and are now incapable of caring for themselves. Thus, the welfare system provides enough money for food, and often provides housing and the other minimum necessities of life.

But the bureaucracy presents one of the greatest problems for democratic socialism. In a somewhat similar way to the problems faced by any bureaucracy, whether in business or in government, it is difficult for the bureaucracy to be as well informed or as responsive to the needs of the people it serves or the industry it serves as would be ideal. Thus, many argue that this large bureaucratic system becomes a tremendous threat to the liberty that the whole democratic socialist system is trying to preserve, because the bureaucracy is not directly responsible to the people. In essence, the democratic socialist system replaces those individuals and groups in the democratic capitalist system who are not held directly accountable to the people. Usually the bureaucracy is composed in large part of full-time employees who are not changed when a government changes, but who remain in their same position and may at times follow policies of their own rather than of the political leaders that are placed at the top of the bureaucracy.

Therefore, democratic socialism at times faces the same problems for which it criticizes democratic capitalism. Still, the democratic socialist would argue that, through their elected representatives, people do have direct control over the bureaucracy and that, when an instance is found in which the bureaucracy is not doing what it is supposed to be doing, the government can immediately change the operations of the bureaucracy.

In many democratic socialist countries, there has been instituted an "ombudsman," whose task is to hear complaints against the bureaucracy and to investigate the complaints and who often has power to make sure that the complaints are corrected. This is a recognition of the problem that the bureaucracies face in any governmental system, because of their size and the needs of the bureaucracy to operate efficiently. These things make it difficult for them to take individual differences into account where they should be taken into account. The operation of the ombudsman in most countries has shown that the majority of the complaints were not well founded but that there have been a significant minority that have indicated lack of concern on the part of the bureaucracies and these complaints have most often been easily corrected.

Thus, the democratic socialist countries have begun to recognize the problem of the bureaucracy and are attempting to correct it. At the same time, there may be some protection for liberty in the relatively independent nature of the bureaucracy. Thus, one bureaucracy may force another bureaucracy to respond better than it would on its own. A case comes to mind in which a university professor from the United States was invited to Canada by a group to give a speech. The immigration official refused him entry into Canada, seemingly because of his pacifist views. The Canadian Broadcasting Company picked up the story and brought it to the attention of the government. Ultimately, the professor was allowed to speak and, rather than speaking to a very small number of people in the original group, he spoke over nationwide television. This illustrates how two bureaucracies, the immigration bureau and the Canadian Broadcasting Company, by coming into conflict, actually helped to protect the liberty and the freedom of the college professor to speak. Of course, this should not have been necessary in the first place but, given the problems that we have noted in bureaucracies, perhaps it is a hopeful sign.

It might be said that the similarities between democratic capitalism and democratic socialism are much greater than are the differences. The differences center on the point of governmental or public ownership of the majority of the important segments of the economy as opposed to private ownership. This central difference is, of course, important and is the focus of the major disagreements between the democratic capitalists and the democratic socialists. The other differences, though, seem to be ones of degree rather than of kind. The extent of the welfare system in democratic socialism is in no place prohibited by democratic capitalist theory. The bureaucracies of the two are also not much different. Both are facing similar problems in the world today. Both democratic socialism and democratic capitalism have produced affluence in various countries, but with affluence, poverty. And the governments of these various countries are attempting to overcome poverty within the dictates of either the capitalist or the socialist system. So far neither one has been very successful.

Democracy and nationalism

One of the peculiarities of all contemporary political ideologies is the manner in which they are each affected by nationalism. Democracy is no exception, although it may be said to affect the practice of countries more than the ideology itself. Usually in the United States, when speaking of the phenomenon known as nationalism, we tend to use *patriotism* when we approve of the action and *nationalism* when we disapprove of the action. Such distinctions are, of course, inherently false since the same type of phenomenon is involved in each case. But the use of the word *patriotism* as an equivalent to *nationalism* should help the American reader to recognize what it is that we are talking about. Americans are familiar with the sort of oratory that is presented to them on the occasion of Fourth of July speeches. Contemporary readers may not be as familiar with the type of nationalism or patriotism that was common earlier in United States history.

Historians speak of a certain period as the period of "manifest destiny." Many people believed that U.S. citizens were, in essence, a chosen people, a people specially selected to rule most if not all of the North American continent and whose example could be the salvation of Europe, which many people believed to be the center of all decadence. Many examples of this feeling can be seen in American history, and similar examples can be found in other democracies, such as that of the United Kingdom. In the United States, we have the example of the desire to save the world for democracy in World War I and at a variety of other times. There is also the current, widespread belief that the United States must act as a world policeman or perhaps a father figure to the rest of the world. And, of course, there is the belief that institutions in the U.S. are somehow better than institutions of other countries, that Americans are more free, more equal, and, on the whole, more democratic and perhaps better than others.

Americans tend to view democracy as something peculiarly American and feel that any nondemocratic institution or any change away from democracy anywhere in the world is somehow a threat to the American system. There is also an intense nationalism or patriotism attached, at least in some circles, to the American economic system. Many people believe that capitalism or the mixed economy, as the economic system in the United States is sometimes called, is better, more just, and certainly more efficient than any other economic system. It is clear that democracies are as prone to nationalism as is any other system or ideology.

The effect of nationalism on democratic ideology seems to center in this belief that democracy is the best system. This is true primarily because Americans tend to equate the United States and democracy. The purer type of nationalism can be found more clearly in other democracies, where there is not quite the same sort of feeling that any threat to democracy is a threat to that particular country. American nationalists tend to believe that the United States must save the world for democracy, particularly from the threat of communism, and they often tend to believe that this must be done with force. This is probably in part also due to the belief in the inherent superiority of capitalism as an economic system; since relatively few countries in the world have a capitalist system, perhaps U.S. capitalists feel somewhat beleaguered or threatened and feel defensive about their system.

Conservatism

Conservatism is many faceted and hence difficult to characterize with any real precision. In the first place what we call conservatism today is composed of three distinct categories. The first, which most conservatives would simply disown, is equivalent to fascism and will be discussed in Chapter 5. The second is an aspect of anarchism and will be discussed in Chapter 8. That leaves democratic conservatism, which again includes a number of significantly different emphases.

One of the most bothersome problems in talking about conservatism in general is its tendency to differ from place to place and time to time. Conservatism is interested, not too surprisingly, in conserving something. But it is difficult to generalize about what it is that conservatives want to conserve because a Canadian conservative will be interested in something different from a Japanese or Swedish conservative. In addition, a conservative in the United States in 1972 does not believe the same things that a U.S. conservative in 1890 did.

Given this problem, we must attempt to avoid, to the extent possible, the time and place limitations and find a characterization of conservatism that will be general enough to fit conservatism at a reasonable number of times and places. At the same time, we must carefully avoid becoming so general as to be meaningless.

Conservatism may best be characterized as follows:

1. Resistance to change
2. Reverence for tradition and a distrust of human reason
3. Rejection of the use of government to improve the human condition—ambivalence regarding governmental activity
4. Favoring individual freedom but willing to limit freedom
5. Anti-egalitarian—distrust of human nature

Now let us look at each of these points.

In an essay entitled, "Why I Am Not a Conservative," F. A. Hayek wrote that "Conservatism proper is a legitimate, probably necessary, and certainly widespread attitude of opposition to drastic change."[29] Although his point is correct, it is too specific. Conservatives not only oppose "drastic change," as he says, but they also are hesitant about any change. As Jay A. Sigler put it, "The conservative does not oppose change, but he does resist it."[30]

Of course, it is possible to find exceptions to this generalization as it is possible to find exceptions to every generalization about conservatism or liberalism. Conservatives *resist* and question change, particularly change for the sake of change since they are wary of social experimentation. They do not unthinkingly oppose change; they *resist* it and question it. They believe that something that has worked, even if not very well, is better than something untried and unknown.

Point two, a "reverence for tradition," is composed of a number of subsidiary points. They include traditional moral standards, religion (with very few exceptions), and generally the assumption that the longer an institution has existed the more likely it is to be worth preserving. This shows

---

[29] F. A. Hayek, "Why I Am Not a Conservative," in *The Constitution of Liberty* (London: Routledge and Kegan Paul, 1960), p. 397.

[30] Jay A. Sigler, "Introduction," in Sigler, ed., *The Conservative Tradition in American Thought* (New York: Capricorn Books, 1969), p. 13.

the conservative's basic distrust of reason as a means of improving man's lot. He does not reject reason completely, but he would rather trust tradition. Note also how closely connected points one and two are—honoring tradition entails resistance to change.

This point is quite simple and clear-cut. The only really complicating factor is that conservatives (and liberals) change over time regarding the specifics they wish to preserve. The world changes and conservatives change with it. They do not want to conserve all the past; they do want to conserve what they see as best in the past.

Point three is the major dilemma in conservative thought. On the whole conservatives believe that governmental power should be reduced and that the individual should make his own way in the world. (Note the similarity to traditional capitalism.) But there is an ambivalence here. Governmental power to support the traditional moral standards and limit an individual's freedom in this realm is perfectly acceptable to conservatives. The conservative seems to be in the unfortunate position of opposing governmental power except when it is on his side.

This is partly because conservatives believe that "genuinely ordered freedom is the only sort of liberty worth having: freedom made possible by order within the soul and order within the state."[31] In other words freedom is good so long as the basic conservative principles are accepted.

But we must not overstate the case. Conservatives basically reject the use of government to improve the human condition. They do this because (1) they are convinced that the use of government does not necessarily help to improve the human condition, and (2) they believe that man left alone can do a better job. The first point is the key one. It asserts that the use of government for social betterment will actually produce the opposite. Men will, according to most conservatives, come to rely on government and lose the ability to help themselves.

Conservatives have held this position very consistently. Edmund Burke writing in the 18th century held it; Bernard Bosanquet writing at the beginning of this century held it; and modern conservatives, such as Russell Kirk still hold it. Men of the better sort will be hurt by governmental help; men of the poorer sort will not be helped.

Conservatives believe that there are men who are better than other men

---

[31] Russell Kirk, "Prescription, Authority, and Ordered Freedom," in Frank S. Meyer, ed., *What Is Conservatism?* (New York: Holt, Rinehart and Winston, 1964), p. 24.

and who, therefore, should be given greater due in society. "Aye, men are created different; and a government which ignores this law becomes an unjust government, for it sacrifices nobility to mediocrity; it pulls down the aspiring natures to gratify the inferior natures."[32] And this is precisely why conservatives are ambivalent about both government and individual freedom.

"The conservative accepts as natural the differences which separate men. Class, intelligence, nationality, and race make men different."[33] This recognition of differences sometimes implies a notion of superiority or inferiority, but it does not necessarily do so. The recognition states that inferiority and superiority exist, but it does not necessarily tie this to such things as race, class, or sex.

These five characteristics are the basic defining characteristics of conservatism. They do not change much over time. The specifics do change, and it would be pointless to try to trace out the details here.[34] Too many writers get lost in the changes that take place in conservatism (and liberalism) and forget the fairly simple principles that characterize both of them.

Liberalism

Liberalism is not as diverse as conservatism. It has a complex history, as does conservatism, and it has played many roles in Western thought, but it does not need to be considered as part of three very different ideologies. Still, it is difficult to pin down precisely because it has the same problem of changing from time to time and place to place that conservatism has. As one scholar has recently noted, "Rather than being a current manifestation of a long intellectual tradition, liberalism, as it is understood today, is largely a product of the twentieth century."[35] It can, though, be characterized in ways that clearly demonstrate its differences from conservatism.

Liberalism can be characterized as follows:

---

[32] Ibid., p. 34.

[33] Sigler, *The Conservative Tradition*, p. 13.

[34] For works that do this to some extent, see ibid. and Peter Viereck, *Conservatism from John Adams to Churchill* (Princeton, N.J.: D. Van Nostrand Co., 1956).

[35] Walter E. Volkomer, "Introduction," in Volkomer, ed., *The Liberal Tradition in American Thought* (New York: Capricorn Books, 1969), p. 1. See the suggested readings at the end of the chapter for a number of opposing interpretations.

1. Having a tendency to favor change
2. Possessing faith in human reason
3. Being willing to use government to improve the human condition
4. Favoring individual freedom
5. Being ambivalent regarding human nature

Now let us look at each of these points.

Hubert H. Humphrey once wrote, "Liberals fully recognize that *change* is inevitable in the patterns of society and in the challenges which confront man."[36] Liberals generally believe that man should keep trying to improve his society. Somewhat less optimistic about progress than it once was, liberalism still believes that beneficial change is possible. This change can come about through man's conscious action, as unforeseen side effects of decisions, or through the operation of various social forces. But there will be change, and the liberal is convinced that it can be directed and controlled for man's benefit.

But they do not desire radical change that does away with the basic structure of the current system. On this point, the difference between liberalism and conservatism is more of degree than of kind. The liberals want more change, tend to welcome change, and tend to favor social experimentation, but they want this only within the framework of the current political, legal, and economic systems. They are not radicals.[37]

Change is accepted because liberals trust the possibilities of human reason to derive solutions to human problems. This faith in the potential of reason is the key to the liberal credo—only with such faith could they accept the use of governmental power to help improve the human condition. And they do believe that such improvement is possible. This faith is not a naive, unquestioning faith, but it assumes that social experimentation is valid and that it is better to use such powers as we have to control change than to simply allow change to come and control us.

Liberals contend that man must and can be helped to live a better life and fulfill his potential as an individual. Conservatives believe just the opposite—helping man will make it impossible for him to fulfill his poten-

---

[36] Hubert H. Humphrey, "Introduction," in Milton Viorst, *Liberalism: A Guide to Its Past, Present and Future in American Politics* (New York: Avon Books, 1963), p. vii. Emphasis in the original.

[37] Arnold S. Kaufman argues that this is changing to some extent. See his *The Radical Liberal: New Man in American Politics* (New York: Atherton Press, 1968).

tial as an individual. Liberals argue that man, though capable of reason and reasoned action, is often caught in situations where self-help, although not impossible, is difficult. At this point the liberal argues that the government should step in and help. They argue that this assistance, far from injuring the man, can (not will) give him the impetus to then do more for himself. The assumption is that, although not everyone will respond, it is better to attempt to help than to do nothing. And in contemporary society, it is believed, only government is in a position to help.

Liberals believe that this help, through governmental activity, will lead to greater individual freedom. Once relieved of some of the basic problems, they argue that man will go on to enlarge his sphere of activity, and improve his life and his mind. Still, liberals are somewhat ambivalent about human nature. They contend that most problems derive from the action of impersonal social and economic forces on man, and they believe that human reason can solve the problems. But they do not believe that the unaided human being can.

The tradition of liberalism most strongly stresses the point of individual freedom. The term liberalism is closely related to liberty, and the emphasis on liberty has been a major thread in all liberal thought. Liberals believe that the individual must be protected and that he must be encouraged to develop his potentials.

The role of the government thus is limited—it cannot invade the rights and freedoms of the individual. Men will err, but liberals have always believed that error is far better than the suppression of error. This belief connects to the belief in the value and inevitability of change. If change is good and will always occur today's error may be tomorrow's truth.

Liberalism and conservatism are both primarily attitudes toward change, resting uneasily between reaction and revolution. Too often attempts are made to transform them into major ideologies with a number of rigidly defined beliefs. This is clearly an error. They do not have these clear-cut beliefs except briefly in response to current problems. They can only be seen as attitudes to change within the democratic tradition.

Contemporary trends

The major recent development in contemporary democratic theory relates to the problem of political participation. Theorists are beginning to argue that the representative system is not working adequately and that the citizenry must be provided with more means of being directly involved in decisions that affect them.[38] Suggestions for the necessary institutional arrangements involved are not easily found—the discussion so far has centered on the need to develop such arrangements rather than on the institutions themselves.

The argument goes somewhat like this. A democratic society is much more than simply a society in which people are allowed to choose periodically who will rule them. A democratic society must be one in which the greatest scope is given to the individual to decide for himself what is good for him. This does not necessarily mean that everything must be decided by the individual alone but that the individual must have the right to participate directly in the making of decisions that affect him. In a modern, complex society, the individual must be consulted on all questions that affect his life; he must not be told what to do or what is right without first being consulted. Clearly, participatory democracy, as this theory is called, leans more toward democratic socialism than toward democratic capitalism, but it is not that simple. The point is that all decisions, economic, political, and social, must gain the consent of people through their participation in the decision-making process.

The defenders of this position say that democracy has merely paid lip service to liberty and equality and these things cannot be achieved without direct participation by those involved. This means that any governmental function should include participation on the part of those it affects.[39]

Another important development that has already been noted and that is related to the demand for participation is the growing position that everyone has a right to a decent standard of living gained from work, not welfare. This position is two-sided. In the first place, the welfare system is rejected, primarily because it has usually been administered in a way that tends to dehumanize the recipient. Second, it is a positive demand that every individual does have a right to life, and to a good life. This assertion has far-reaching implications for the democratic societies that have for so

---

[38] An excellent plea for greater political participation is made by Henry S. Kariel in *The Promise of Politics* (Englewood Cliffs, N.J.: Prentice-Hall, 1967), and his *Open Systems; Arenas for Political Action* (Itasca, Ill.: F. E. Peacock Publishers, 1969).

[39] See Chapter 7, "The New Left," for more material on this topic.

long been preaching liberty and equality and at the same time denying it to so many.

A final development is the questioning that a number of thinkers are now directing at the viability of large countries, such as the United States, as democracies. Even with our tremendously sophisticated communications technology, can an individual be expected to actively participate in the day-to-day life of so large a country. And, since we must recognize the fact that for the time being at least we have such large countries, if so, how? No answers have yet been given. Democratic theory is still developing.

Suggested readings

The principles of democracy

Adler, Mortimer J. *The Idea of Freedom; A Dialectical Examination of the Conceptions of Freedom.* New York: Doubleday, 1958.

Bay, Christian. *The Structure of Freedom.* Stanford, Calif.: Stanford University Press, 1958.

Braybrooke, David. *Three Tests for Democracy, Personal Rights, Human Welfare, Collective Preference.* New York: Random House, 1968.

Dahl, Robert A. *A Preface to Democratic Theory.* Chicago: University of Chicago Press, 1956.

Hallowell, John H. *The Moral Foundation of Democracy.* Chicago: University of Chicago Press, 1954.

Macpherson, C. B. *The Real World of Democracy.* Oxford, Eng.: Clarendon Press, 1966.

Mayo, Henry B. *An Introduction to Democratic Theory.* New York: Oxford University Press, 1960.

Oppenheim, Felix E. *Dimensions of Freedom; An Analysis.* New York: St. Martin's Press, 1961.

Riemer, Neal. *The Revival of Democratic Theory.* New York: Appleton-Century-Crofts, 1962.

Sartori, Giovanni. *Democratic Theory.* New York: Frederick A. Praeger, 1965.

Simon, Yves. *Philosophy of Democratic Government.* Chicago: University of Chicago Press, 1951.

Thorson, Thomas Landon. *The Logic of Democracy.* New York: Holt, Rinehart & Winston, 1962.

Democratic capitalism

Berle, Adolf A., Jr. *The 20th Century Capitalist Revolution.* New York: Harcourt, Brace & Co., 1954.

Chase, Harold W., and Dolan, Paul. *The Case for Democratic Capitalism.* New York: Thomas Y. Crowell, 1964.

Tipple, John. *The Capitalist Revolution; A History of American Social Thought 1890–1919.* New York: Pegasus, 1970.

Democratic socialism

Crosland, C. A. R. *The Future of Socialism.* New York: Schocken Books, 1963.

Crossman, R. H. S. (ed.). *New Fabian Essays.* London: Turnstile Press, 1952.

Thomas, Norman. *Socialism Re-examined.* New York: W. W. Norton & Co., 1963.

Conservatism

Hayek, Friedrich A. *The Constitution of Liberty.* London: Routledge & Kegan Paul, 1960.

———. *The Road to Serfdom.* Chicago: University of Chicago Press, 1944.

———. *Studies in Philosophy, Politics and Economics.* Chicago: University of Chicago Press, 1967.

Kendall, Willmoore. *The Conservative Affirmation.* Chicago: Henry Regnery Co., 1954.

Kirk, Russell. *A Program for Conservatives.* Chicago: Henry Regnery Co., 1954.

Meyer, Frank S. (ed.). *What is Conservatism?* New York: Holt, Rinehart & Winston, 1964.

Sigler, Jay A. (ed.) *The Conservative Tradition in American Thought.* New York: Capricorn Books, 1969.

Smith, Dean. *Conservatism: A Guide to its Past, Present and Future in American Politics.* New York: Avon Books, 1963.

Viereck, Peter. *Conservatism: From John Adams to Churchill.* Princeton, N.J.: D. Van Nostrand Co., 1956.

Liberalism

De Ruggiero, Guido. *The History of European Liberalism.* Trans. R. G. Collingwood. Boston: Beacon Press, 1959.

Girvetz, Harry K. *The Evolution of Liberalism.* New York: Collier Books, 1963.

Kaufman, Arnold S. *The Radical Liberal; New Man in American Politics.* New York: Atherton Press, 1968.

Laski, Harold J. *The Rise of European Liberalism: An Essay in Interpretation.* London: George Allen & Unwin, 1936.

Schapiro, J. Salwyn. *Liberalism: Its Meaning and History.* Princeton, N.J.: D. Van Nostrand Co., 1958.

Spitz, David. *Essays in the Liberal Idea of Freedom.* Tucson: The University of Arizona Press, 1964.

Viorst, Milton. *Liberalism; A Guide to its Past, Present and Future in American Politics.* New York: Avon Books. 1963.

Volkomer, Walter E. (ed.) *The Liberal Tradition in American Thought.* New York: Capricorn Books, 1969.

Contemporary trends

Harrington, Michael. *Toward a Democratic Left; A Radical Program for a New Majority.* New York: Macmillan Co., 1968.

Howe, Irving. *Steady Work: Essays in the Politics of Democratic Radicalism 1953–1966.* New York: Harcourt, Brace & World, 1966.

Kariel, Henry S. *Open Systems; Arenas for Political Action.* Itasca, Ill.: F. E. Peacock Publishers, 1969.

———. *The Promise of Politics.* Englewood Cliffs, N.J.: Prentice-Hall, 1967.

5

FASCISM AND
NATIONAL SOCIALISM

For the generation that lived through World War II, the words *fascism, national socialism,* and *nazism* raise indescribably horrible pictures of brutality and inhumanity. For those who have grown up since the end of the war, the horror associated with the concentration camps has faded somewhat. The word *fascist* is currently used by many to describe anyone of conservative political view or even any member of the establishment. While attributing fascist views to such people is almost always inaccurate, fascism and national socialism are far from dead. In fact, it seems that they are reviving in many countries.

Fascism and national socialism are similar enough to be called one ideology. There are differences, but national socialism is more accurately seen as a subtype of fascism rather than different in kind. Furthermore, we tend to identify them with two different men—Benito Mussolini with fascism and Adolf Hitler with national socialism—and this distinction is important. From the standpoint of the theorist, Mussolini is the more important man; from the standpoint of the history of the 20th century, Hitler dominates the picture. Identifying fascism with Mussolini is inaccurate, but not fatally so. Identifying national socialism with Hitler is very nearly correct. The differences in the varieties of fascism are due in large part to (1) the different personalities of the leaders and (2) the differences among the countries involved, due in large part to nationalism. But such identifications are not *completely* correct because fascism is a broader political ideology than is represented by any particular individual or nation.

107

Nevertheless, it should be kept in mind that, although national socialism can best be seen as a subtype of fascism predominantly identified with the personality of Hitler, it did not die with him. National socialism has adherents today who are attempting to develop a movement on the basis of the ideas that they find in the writings of other National Socialists, and Hitler in particular, but who do not identify themselves solely with Hitler. Hitler is seen as an early great leader of the movement but only as this and not as a figure whose word must be taken without question. Therefore, in analyzing national socialism as a subtype of fascism, we must attempt to get beyond the personality of Hitler to the ideas that make up this ideology and see in what respects fascism and national socialism do differ.

The theoretical base

Any discussion of fascism and national socialism must emphasize six basic concepts that are found in all Fascists and National Socialists. Although the concepts are given different emphases by different writers, they all exist in all the writers. They are:

1. Irrationalism
2. Social Darwinism
3. Nationalism
4. The totalitarian state
5. The principle of leadership
6. Racism (more important in national socialism than in fascism)

The first two concepts are best seen as basic themes that are rarely explicitly stated but which are part of the other four. All six of these concepts are intimately interrelated, and the reader should avoid placing each in a separate compartment cut off from the others. But it is necessary to analyze them separately to understand them.

Irrationalism.[1]   The irrational is a very difficult notion to grasp. We are accustomed in Western thought to speak of man in terms of the rational rather than the irrational. We are seldom entirely sure what we mean when we speak of the rational, and we are even less sure of the meaning of the word *irrational*. But, in the context of fascism and national socialism, it is possible to get a glimpse of what is meant by the irrationality of man

---

[1] Irrationalism is also part of other ideologies, but it is most important in relationship to fascism and national socialism.

within this one ideology and its subtype. Fascism and national socialism assume that men are part of a mass. This is more than saying that men are members of a community: it is the idea that a man is thoroughly conditioned by his existence in a particular society. In the conditioning that takes place, there are certain beliefs that he shares with all others in the society at a level where they are not likely to be consciously recognized. These beliefs and values can be triggered by an appeal to certain fears and emotions that brings them to the surface. They are notions of race, blood, and soil, ideas arising out of man's emotional and fearful side. They allow him to hate, and they allow him to be controlled and manipulated by people who recognize these fears and hates and who know how to release them. The technique is to appeal to the lowest level in man, and, as Hitler often indicated, in order to sway a crowd, no matter what its composition, all you have to do is appeal to the lowest common denominator in the crowd, and you can get the crowd with you and be able to manipulate it. Fascism and national socialism recognized and used this man, made up of fear and hate, to build the basis of their movement.

Social Darwinism.   Social Darwinism is the name generally given to social theories that view life as a struggle for survival within each species as well as between the species. In Charles Darwin's[2] book *On the Origin of Species by Means of Natural Selection* (1859), there is found the statement that life evolved through a struggle for survival *between* the species. The Social Darwinists took this idea and applied it to each species. In other words, rather than seeing a struggle for survival *between* the species, they saw a struggle for survival *within* the species.[3] Fascists and National Socialists applied the idea to their theories of nationalism and race, and we will return to it in that context. It should be clear from the above that not all Social Darwinists are racists. Social Darwinism is a general theory that the Fascists and National Socialists applied to their theories.

Nationalism.   By far the most important theme, as illustrated in the phrase *national socialism,* is nationalism. In Chapter 2 we analyzed the basic characteristics of nationalism. Here we will try to see what they mean

---

[2] Charles Darwin (1809–1882). Famous English naturalist who put forth a number of important theses regarding evolution.

[3] A later thinker whom we will look at in the chapter on "Anarchism," Peter Kropotkin (1842–1921), argues in his book *Mutual Aid* (1902) that there is considerable evidence for cooperation within the species.

to the Fascist. A good beginning to understanding nationalism in this context can be found in Hitler's statement, "I am deeply stirred by the word which Ulrich Hutten wrote the last time he seized his pen:—Germany."[4] Here we find the fundamental notion of nationalism as patriotism or love of country, but, in fascism, nationalism is much more than this simple statement. It takes on a much different meaning, to the extent that some scholars call it by a modified name, such as "integral" nationalism.[5]

Nationalism for the Fascist and the National Socialist is one aspect of the mass mind or mass society that we mentioned in connection with the irrational. It is, in addition, more than that for the Fascist for whom the nation is the key unit to which one is related. For the National Socialist, this position is most often taken by race, with the nation as a secondary concern rather than the primary one. An individual is for the Fascist first and foremost a member of the nation. The nation is that thing to which he gives all of his loyalty, all of his dedication, and all of his love. The individual cannot exist separate from his existence in the nation. In this way, there is essentially no such thing as an individual within Fascist ideology. An individual is one small part of the nation.

This feeling of being part of the nation goes beyond Doob's definition of nationalism. It is much closer to his specific definition of patriotism than it is to his definition of nationalism. For the Fascist, nationalism does not give rise to something within the individual. The individual and the nation are inseparable. The individual should not be able to conceive of himself as something different from his existence in the nation. He should be completely wrapped up in the nation. Therefore, he would be unable to conceive of the nation going out of existence, and demands made on this basis would seem rather pointless to him. Although not all citizens of Fascist countries felt this strongly, it does illustrate the ideal Fascist citizen. The Fascist citizen would think like this if he completely fitted the mold of the ideology. Certainly, there will be very few individuals who completely fit that mold, but one must remember again the underlying motif of the irrational in Fascist ideology, particularly since this love of nation, this nationalism, was consciously used by the leadership to mold the citizens as close to the model as possible. For the Fascist the nation was the key

---

[4] Quoted in A. P. Laurie, *The Case for Germany: A Study of Modern Germany* (Berlin: Internationaler Verlag, 1939), p. 2.

[5] See, for example, Carlton J. H. Hayes, *The Historical Evolution of Modern Nationalism* (New York: Macmillan Co., 1931), pp. 164–231.

to this molding. For the National Socialist it was race, but it was race closely connected with nation.

For the National Socialist, nationalism was usually so closely connected with racism that it formed one concept rather than two. This is neatly illustrated by the following directive to all German schools:

Teachers are directed to instruct their pupils in "the nature, causes, and effects of all racial and hereditary problems," to bring home to them the importance of race and heredity for the life and destiny of the German people, and to awaken in them a sense of their responsibility toward "the community of the nation" (their ancestors, the present generation, and posterity), pride in their membership of the German race as a foremost vehicle of hereditary Nordic values, and the will consciously to cooperate in the racial purification of the German stock. Racial instruction is to begin with the youngest pupils (six years of age) in accordance with the desire of the Führer "that no boy or girl should leave school without complete knowledge of the necessity and meaning of blood purity."[6]

Here we see the intimate connection in Nazi thought between racism and nationalism, and we see an explicit attempt to use the educational system to give children the value system of the ideology.

But, for the Fascist in general, racism is not closely connected to nationalism. In fact, racism, although part of the Fascist outlook, played a fairly minor role in both ideology and practice in a number of countries, such as Italy. In other countries with Fascist groups today, racism is an important part of the ideology. The United States is one of these countries with a number of small groups on the extreme right wing of the political spectrum that are either National Socialist or Fascist and racist and who often view themselves as descendents of Hitler.

Nonracist fascism does hold a strongly nationalist position, but it is usually presented in connection with the concept of the state. The following statement by Mussolini is a good example: "The key-stone of the Fascist doctrine is the conception of the State, of its essence, of its functions, its aims. For Fascism the State is absolute, individuals and groups relative."[7] Mussolini continues in the same vein, contending that the state is the

---

[6] Quoted in *The Times* (London), 29 January 1935, p. 12, reprinted by permission of *The Times.* Also reprinted in George L. Mosse, *Nazi Culture: Intellectual, Cultural and Social Life in the Third Reich* (New York: Grosset & Dunlap, 1966), pp. 282–84.

[7] Benito Mussolini, "The Doctrine of Fascism," in Mussolini, *Fascism; Doctrine and Institutions* (New York: Howard Fertig, 1968), p. 27.

carrier of the culture and spirit of the people or nation; that it is the past, present, and future[8]; that it represents the "immanent conscience of the nation"; and that it educates the citizens in all the virtues.[9] Here we have clearly stated the connection between the state and nationalism in Fascist ideology. Mussolini's statements on the role of the state illustrate that the state should be seen as the physical embodiment of the spirit of the nation. The state is that entity which brings together the ideas and ideals that form the basis of nationalism. In this sense nationalism and the notion of the state cannot be easily separated for the Fascist. The state is that entity which brings about the ideals of the nation. The state, as Mussolini said, is the carrier of the culture and spirit of the people. The state is the driving force that welds together the people. The state is capable of focusing the spirit of the people and the nationalism of the country. The state for these reasons must be strong. The state must have the power necessary to weld these things together. Therefore, the state is closely connected to the principle of leadership that we will look at shortly.

The totalitarian state.[10]   The role of the state in Fascist ideology is illustrated by its connection with nationalism, but it is also significant by itself. The notion of the state in both fascism and national socialism is at least verbally complex, if not actually so. As Hitler put it:

> Men do not exist for the State, the State exists for men. First and far above all else stands the idea of the people: the State is a form of organization of this people, and the meaning and the purpose of the State are through this form of organization to assure the life . . . of the people.[11]

It should be noted that in this statement Hitler nowhere refers in any way to the individual; he refers to man and he refers to the people. We noted

---

[8] Note the close similarity to Edmund Burke.

[9] Ibid., pp. 27–28.

[10] The student who is interested in the theories of dictatorship and totalitarianism should refer to Betty Brand Burch, ed., *Dictatorship and Totalitarianism; Selected Readings* (Princeton, N.J.: D. Van Nostrand Co., 1964); Hannah Arendt, *The Origins of Totalitarianism*, new ed. (New York: Harcourt, Brace and Jovanovich, 1966); Carl J. Friedrich, ed., *Totalitarianism* (New York: Grosset & Dunlap, 1954); Carl J. Friedrich and Zbigniew K. Brzezinski, *Totalitarian Dictatorship and Autocracy*, 2nd ed. (Cambridge, Mass.: Harvard University Press, 1965); and Carl J. Friedrich, Michael Curtis, and Benjamin R. Barber, *Totalitarianism in Perspective: Three Views* (New York: Frederick A. Praeger, 1969), particularly the essay by Barber.

[11] Adolf Hitler, *The Speeches of Adolf Hitler, April 1922–August 1939*, Norman H. Baynes, ed. (London: Oxford University Press, 1942), vol. I, p. 187. Speech of September, 1930.

earlier that Fascists and National Socialists do not think in terms of individuals. They think in terms of masses.

If there is a central concept around which a thorough analysis of fascism and national socialism can be built, it is the idea of the state. Although nationalism, or the nation, is usually stressed by all Fascist and National Socialist writers, the state is the vehicle through which the attributes of the nation, nationality, or the race are expressed. But, to understand the distinction they make, it should be noted that the state, at least as viewed by Hitler, is a "rigid formal organization," and the nation or the people is a "living organism," which must replace the state.[12] The theory of the state as actually presented by Fascists and National Socialists combines these two notions into the idea of an organic[13] or corporate state.

This conception of the state stresses the continuity over the generations of the entire society. The word *organic* means that "social groups as fractions of the species receive thereby a life and scope which transcends the scope and life of the individuals identifying themselves with the history and finalities of the uninterrupted series of generations."[14] Put somewhat differently, this means that the society, represented by the state, is a separate entity having a life or existence at once different from, and more than, the life of any individual within that society. This also means that the life of the individual is less important than the life of the society.

This point, which we have mentioned before, is best illustrated by the idea of the folkish state that we find expressed by Hitler in *Mein Kampf*:

Thus, the highest purpose of a *folkish* state is concern for the preservation of those original racial elements which bestow culture and create the beauty and dignity of a higher mankind. We, as Aryans, can conceive of the state only as the living organism of a nationality which not only assures the preservation of this nationality, but by the development of its spiritual and ideal abilities leads it to the highest freedom.[15]

The folkish state is the best symbol that one can find for the full idea of the loss of the individual in the mass. The National Socialist would not, of

---

[12] Ibid., p. 188. Speech of September, 1930.

[13] Fascists reject the idea that they are presenting the "organic theory of the state." See, for example, Alfredo Rocco, "The Political Doctrine of Fascism," in *Readings on Fascism and National Socialism* (Denver, Colo.: Alan Swallow, Publisher, n.d.), p. 34.

[14] Ibid.

[15] Adolf Hitler, *Mein Kampf,* trans., Ralph Manheim (Boston: Houghton Mifflin Co., 1943), p. 394. Emphasis in the original.

course, consider this a loss, but rather a gain. Be that as it may, the folkish state is the true embodiment of this idea. Here we have the ideas of blood and soil intermingled in a way that illustrates why they are so important to national socialism. The folkish state is a racial state. It is a state in which only the members of the true Aryan race may participate, but they participate only in the sense of giving of themselves to the state. They do not participate in any sense of governing. The folkish state, then, is a state based on racial purity. Furthermore, it is a state based on ideas of soil, myths of racial content, but connected with the particular history of the German nation in this case. Here we have race and nationalism, blood and soil, combined in the notion of the folkish state.

It is clear, therefore, that an understanding of national socialism as it developed in Germany cannot be separated from an understanding of race, nationalism, and the combination of the two in a folkish state. Here it is important to note that there is a difference between the National Socialist and the Fascist conceptions of the state. It is a difference primarily of emphasis rather than of content, but it is a significantly different emphasis.

The theory of the corporate state is found, if somewhat obscurely, in Mussolini. He specifically rejects Hitler's position that the nation is prior to the state. It should also be noted that the reason that Mussolini rejects Hitler's idea that the nation is more important than the state is the very simple one that Mussolini is arguing that the nation cannot exist without the state to weld together the disparate masses into a nation. Mussolini says that the state is the source of the life of the people of all generations that compose it.[16] The state is owed supreme loyalty by the individuals who live within it at any particular time, but the state is also something more than these somewhat mechanical notions imply. The state is also a "spiritual" unit, but this "spiritual" side is closely related to the authority that controls the state at any given time. The state ". . . enforces discipline and uses authority, entering into the soul and ruling with undisputed sway."[17] This is, of course, the leadership principle noted earlier in the writings of Hitler.

The leadership principle. The state is the mechanism for enforcing the Fascist beliefs, and the state is run on the leadership or *Führer* princi-

---

[16] Mussolini, "The Doctrine of Fascism," pp. 11–12.
[17] Ibid., p. 14.

ple which states that each subordinate owes absolute obedience to his immediate superior, with everyone ultimately subordinate to the absolute leader, the *Führer*. This hierarchy of leaders with a single, absolute leader at the top is an important characteristic of fascism and national socialism, although it should be noted that the underlying theory contends that the *Führer* is not absolute. But the only limit on his power, even in the theory, is that he must reflect the collective will of the people. This in no way actually limits the power of the leader even in the theory because his will is defined as being the same as the collective will. "His will is not the subjective, individual will of a single man, but the collective national will. . . ."[18] The leader's authority, therefore, in national socialism and, for the same reason, in fascism is absolute.

The *Führer* principle on which Hitler based his power and organization seems, on the surface, to be somewhat complicated, but, if we remember the discussion of representation in the chapter on democracy, we will recall the notion of the representative as embodying within himself the will of his constituency. This is what is meant by the *Führer* principle. Hitler, as leader, is the representative of the German nation and of the Aryan race in the sense that he embodies within himself all the aspirations of the people. It should be clear that this does not mean that Hitler follows the will of the people, but that he, by embodying their will, is capable of *rightly* interpreting it. This is the clue to the whole notion of the *Führer* principal—the *Führer* is the only one who is capable of rightly interpreting the will of the people. When the *Führer* speaks, he speaks as the representative of what the people truly want. In this sense he must be considered to be virtually infallible, and this is clearly how Hitler viewed himself. Hitler as *Führer* could not err.

But one man cannot rule an entire country, even if his will is the embodiment of the collective will of the people of that country, and therefore even an absolute ruler needs some apparatus to enforce his rules. This apparatus is found in the party. Party members are the most direct participants in the leader-follower relationship defined above, and they all are apart from and above the population as a whole. They are also normally identified by some clearly recognizable sign, such as a uniform. Finally,

---

[18] Ernst Rudolf Huber, *Verfassungsrecht des grossdeutschen Reiches* (Hamburg, 1939), p. 195; trans. and quoted in *Readings on Fascism and National Socialism*, p. 75.

there is often an elite corps within this elite which serves in part to check on the rest of the party. The two groups who served this function within the National Socialist German Workers party (the official name of Hitler's party) were the S.A. (*Sturmabteilung*) and the S.S. (*Schutzstaffel*). Hitler defined the task of the S.A. as follows:

The SA on behalf of our German people must educate the young German in mind and body so that he becomes a man hard as steel and ready to fight.

Out of hundreds of thousands of individuals it must forge one united, disciplined, mighty organization.

In the age of Democracy and authority of the Leader, in the period of unbridled freedom, iron discipline, must be the foundation of the SA.[19]

This statement is also illustrative of the role of the entire party. It is expected to obey without question, and its primary task is to educate the entire population in the correct principles of life.

Under Hitler the party is the effective ruling mechanism. As Hitler said:

The function of the State is the continuance of the administration, as it has in the course of history arisen and developed, of the State-organizations within the framework of and by means of the law.

The function of the Party is:

1. The building up of its own internal organization so as to create a stable, self-renewing, permanent cell of National Socialist teaching.
2. The education of the entire people in the meaning of the conceptions of this idea.
3. The introduction of those who have been so trained into the State to serve either as leaders or followers. . . .[20]

But lest there be any mistake as to what this means, he also says, "With us the Leader and the idea are one, and every member of the Party has to do what the leader orders."[21]

The party in fascism and national socialism played a role similar to that of the Communist party in Lenin's thought. The party was seen as the vanguard of the nation or the race rather than the proletariat, but the general notion is the same. The party is the forerunner of the new order to

---

[19] Adolf Hitler, "Introduction to the Service-Order of the S.A.," quoted in Hitler, *Speeches*, vol. I, p. 169.

[20] Hitler, *Speeches*, vol. I., p. 444. Speech of 1935.

[21] Ibid., p. 459. Speech of May 21, 1930.

come. For the Nationalist Socialist as opposed to the Fascist, the new order is based on race.

Racism. Probably the single, best-known part of national socialism is its racism. Hitler's refusal to award the Olympic gold medal to the Negro athlete Jesse Owen in the 1936 Olympics in Berlin is a well-known example of this attitude. Everyone also knows of the killing of six million Jews in Nazi Germany, and we have to struggle to understand the belief system that lies behind this. It is not the purpose of this book to analyze the causes of prejudice and racism,[22] but only to attempt to understand their role within an ideology.

Hitler bases racism originally on the right of the stronger,[23] and he believed that from the very beginning the Aryan, or Nordic, or white, or sometimes German, race dominated all others. He contended that this domination was good for all because it was natural and founded on reason, and also that it was ultimately accepted gladly by the dominated races.[24]

Here we have clearly stated the thesis of the struggle for survival among the races. It is noteworthy that Hitler believed that racial domination by the Aryans would in fact gladly be accepted by the dominated races. This clearly is rationalization of his basic belief. The Darwinian notion of struggle for survival as interpreted by the National Socialist does not in fact necessarily include the survival of the dominated races. The logic of the position is that the inferior races will be eliminated, not merely dominated. The only situation in which the dominated races could in fact continue to exist would be the situation in which it was felt that certain menial tasks required races lower than the Aryans to fulfill them. This notion reminds one of Aldous Huxley's *Brave New World* (1932), where specific differences were bred among men so that the various groups would be happy doing what they had to do. Only in this sense could Hitler's idea that the dominated races would accept gladly their domination possibly be valid.

Again, we should be very careful to note the role that racism plays in national socialism. It represents (1) the underlying current of Social Darwinism and (2) it was a mechanism of social control negatively by destroy-

---

[22] See the following studies for works on this problem: Gordon W. Allport, *The Nature of Prejudice* (Garden City, N.Y.: Doubleday & Co., 1958), and Edgar T. Thompson and Everett C. Hughes, eds., *Race: Individual and Collective Behavior* (Glencoe, Ill.: Free Press, 1958).

[23] Hitler, *Speeches*, vol. I, p. 465. Speech of January 15, 1936.

[24] Ibid., pp. 465–66.

ing the Jews and thus instilling fear in the Germans and positively by instilling a pride in the Germans in their so-called racial heritage. The racial policies of Hitler were not limited to extermination and breeding. They extended to the argument that all that is good in culture stems from the Aryan race and that, therefore, the Germans as the representatives of the Aryans had the best cultural heritage of the Western world and would have an even better culture in the future. In the chapter on nationalism we noted that one of Hitler's great loves was Wagner. This was true because Wagner's operas were in some ways operas of the folkish state. They represented the myths of blood and soil that were so important to national socialism. Most importantly, they represented what Hitler saw as a high point in German culture—an illustration that the Germans did in fact have a great culture and particularly that Wagner, as a representative of German culture, seemed to agree in large part with the ideas put forth by Hitler. Therefore, Hitler could present national socialism as a logical outgrowth of German culture and the German nation.

The relationship of the state to racism is seen in the following extract from *Mein Kampf*:

> The state is a means to an end. Its end lies in the preservation and advancement of a community of physically and psychically homogeneous creatures. This preservation itself comprises first of all existence as a race and thereby permits the free development of all the forces dormant in this race. Of them a part will always primarily serve the preservation of physical life, and only the remaining part the promotion of a further spiritual development. Actually the one always creates the precondition for the other.[25]

The social system

In an ideology based on an elite rule and racism, certain of the other parts of the ideology are fairly simple and obvious. For example, social stratification would be based on racial purity and party membership. Other things that would be taken into account would be positive support for the regime and contributions to the country. Social mobility would be largely based on party membership. In addition, the racist ideology would dictate control of marriage, and the desire to control the minds of the children would dictate control of the family system. Along these lines, the

---

[25] Hitler, *Mein Kampf*, p. 393.

German woman was encouraged to have many children, that is, if she was of the correct racial type. As Goebbels put it, "The mission of woman is to be beautiful and to bring children into the world."[26] She is also supposed to be athletic and refrain from wearing makeup or from such things as smoking in public. But, above all, she is to have children. We have seen the way in which the educational system was used to develop the correct values in the children. The family and religion were used in the same way. Parents were supposed to teach their children the correct National Socialist ideas from birth. National socialism also contended that it was supported by God, and thus religion was used for the same purpose.

The final aspect of the social system, the economic system, is the most difficult to treat because the theory is inconsistent. Even though socialism is part of the name national socialism and Mussolini was originally a socialist, neither fascism nor national socialism was actually socialist. National socialism began from that position, but it quickly changed as it gained the support of capitalists.[27] Probably the best statement of the general economic theory is Huber's:

> All property is common property. The owner is bound by the people and the Reich to the responsible management of his goods. His legal position is only justified when he satisfies this responsibility to the community.[28]

Thus, property under national socialism was held in private hands, but it had to be used as the government dictated or it would be confiscated.

Here again we have the idea of the people as a whole acting for unity. The economic system of national socialism clearly states that, even though an individual may have temporary control of some economic good, be it land or capital or whatever, this control must serve the interests of the collectivity as interpreted by the *Führer* or the control must be terminated.

The economic system of fascism as distinct from that of national socialism more clearly incorporates this idea of state-controlled syndicates. The state creates all economic organizations as the Labor Charter of April 21, 1927 says:

---

[26] Joseph Goebbels, quoted in Mosse, *Nazi Culture*, p. 41.

[27] On this point see Martin Broszat, *German National Socialism 1919–1945*, trans., Kurt Rosenbaum and Inge Pauli Boehm (Santa Barbara, Calif.: CLIO Press, 1966), pp. 22–24.

[28] Huber, *Verfassungsrecht*, pp. 327–73, quoted in *Readings on Facism*, p. 91.

Work in all its forms—intellectual, technical and manual—both organizing or executive, is a social duty. On this score and only on this score, it is protected by the State.

From the national standpoint the mass of production represents a single unit; it has a single object, namely the well-being of individuals and the development of national power.[29]

All economic organization under fascism is created by the state. All economic organizations under fascism are designed to include both workers and the employers in the same organization so that all of the economy can be directly controlled from above. In this way the state is made clearly superior to every part of the economy. The syndicates are designed to insure that production continues as long as the state requires it. The right to strike is taken away from the workers, but at the same time the syndicate operating as an arm of the state usually has the power to set wages, and thus the syndicate acts as a policy-making arm of the state in economic affairs. It should be clear that, as in Germany, the Fascist party in Italy with Mussolini at the head of it had ultimate power. In many ways, the syndicates were merely administrative arms of the Fascist party and of Mussolini rather than having any real power to make decisions. The leadership principle was not abrogated in Italy. It was maintained, and the syndicates acted as lower-level leaders following the dictates of the leader.

The current scene

Evidence regarding the current status of fascism and national socialism around the world is spotty to say the least. One often reads of the resurgence of these movements in Germany and Japan, and, until the assassination of George Lincoln Rockwell, the Nazi party in the United States got considerable press coverage, even though its membership was very small.

The greatest difficulty in analyzing the current situation stems from the tendency for movements to reject the labels of fascism or national socialism and for the number of adherents to be relatively small and thus not attract much attention. They seem, therefore, to be unimportant. At the same time, we must remember that the movements founded by Hitler and

---

[29] "The Labour Charter," in Benito Mussolini, *Four Speeches on the Corporate State* (Rome: "Laboremus," 1935), p. 53.

Mussolini began in obscurity and were very small for many years. Thus, one cannot say with any certainty that a major Fascist or National Socialist movement is impossible. One can only say that such a movement is unlikely without certain conditions being present that give rise to considerable unrest, dissatisfaction, and demands for order. Such conditions obviously do exist in some countries, including the United States. It is possible that popular leaders could arise in any number of countries and achieve success through National Socialist or Fascist movements whether or not the actual label was used.

For such a movement to be successful, it will clearly require something more than simply dissatisfaction and demands for order. It will require an issue with great emotional content. This issue is certainly present today in the United States in the question of race. Other issues can be made to have such emotional content with the appropriate type of leader. Thus, it would be a mistake to think of national socialism and fascism as dead, even though no major movements seem to exist.

In conclusion, I would like to simply quote from a recent survey of fascism. "Fascism and Nazism are still with us. Regimes and organizations inspired by them, or using the methods they have made all too famous, are still operating in all the five continents."[30]

Suggested readings

Baumont, Maurice; Fried, John H. E.; and Vermeil, Edmond (eds.). The Third Reich. New York: Frederick A. Praeger, 1954.

Blanksten, George I. Peron's Argentina. New York: Russell & Russell, 1953.

Broszat, Martin. German National Socialism, 1919–1945. Trans. Kurt Rosenbaum and Inge Pauli Boehm. Santa Barbara, Calif.: CLIO Press, 1966.

Carsten, F. L. The Rise of Fascism. Berkeley: University of California Press, 1967.

Chabod, Federico. A History of Italian Fascism. London: Weidenfeld, 1963.

Del Boca, Angelo, and Giovana, Mario. Fascism Today; A World Survey. Trans. R. H. Boothroyd. New York: Pantheon Books, 1969.

Ebenstein, William. Fascist Italy. New York: American Book Co., 1939.

———. The Nazi State. New York: Farrar, 1943.

Fermi, Laura. Mussolini. Chicago: University of Chicago Press, 1961.

---

[30] Angelo Del Boca and Mario Giovana, Fascism Today; A World Survey, trans., R. H. Boothroyd (New York: Pantheon Books, 1969), p. 428.

Germino, Dante L. *The Italian Fascist Party in Power: A Study in Totalitarian Rule.* Minneapolis: University of Minnesota Press, 1959.

Gregor, A. James. *The Ideology of Fascism; The Rationale of Totalitarianism.* New York: The Free Press, 1969.

Halperin, S. William (ed.). *Mussolini and Italian Fascism.* Princeton, N.J.: D. Van Nostrand Co., 1964.

Harris, Henry Silton. *The Social Philosophy of Giovanni Gentile.* Urbana: University of Illinois Press, 1960.

Hitler, Adolf. *Mein Kampf.* Trans. Ralph Manheim. Boston: Houghton Mifflin Co., 1943.

――――. *My New Order.* New York: Reynal & Hitchcock, 1941.

――――. *The Speeches of Adolf Hitler.* Ed. Norman H. Baynes. 2 vols. London: Oxford University Press, 1942.

Laquer, Walter, and Mosse, George L. (eds.). *International Fascism 1920–1945.* New York: Harper & Row, 1966. First published as Vol. I, No. 1, of the *Journal of Contemporary History.*

Laurie, A. P. *The Case for Germany; A Study of Modern Germany.* Berlin: Internationaler Verlag, 1939.

Mosse, George L. *The Crisis of German Ideology; Intellectual Origins of the Third Reich.* New York: Grosset & Dunlap, 1964.

――――. *Nazi Culture; Intellectual, Cultural and Social Life in the Third Reich.* New York: Grosset & Dunlap, 1966.

Mussolini, Benito. *The Corporate State.* Florence, Italy: Vallecchi, 1936.

――――. *Fascism: Doctrine and Institutions.* New York: Howard Fertig, 1968.

――――. *Four Speeches on the Corporate State.* Rome: "Laboremus," 1935.

――――. *My Autobiography.* New York: Charles Scribner's Sons, 1928.

Neumann, Franz. *Behemoth: The Structure and Practice of National Socialism.* 2nd ed. New York: Octagon Books, 1963.

Nolte, Ernst. *Three Faces of Fascism: Action Francaise, Italian Fascism, National Socialism.* Trans. Leila Vennewitz. New York: Holt, Rinehart & Winston, 1965.

Payne, Stanley G. *Falange; A History of Spanish Fascism.* Stanford, Calif.: Stanford University Press, 1961.

Readings on Fascism and National Socialism. Denver, Colo.: Alan Swallow, Publisher, n.d.

Rocco, Alfredo. "Political Doctrine of Fascism." Trans. D. Bigongiari. *International Conciliation,* No. 223 (October, 1926), pp. 393–415.

Rogger, Hans, and Weber, Eugen (eds.). *The European Right; A Historical Profile.* Berkeley: University of California Press, 1965.

Silone, Ignazio. *The School for Dictators.* Trans. William Wiever. New York: Atheneum, 1963.

Speer, Albert. *Inside the Third Reich: Memoirs.* Trans. Richard and Clara Winston. New York: Macmillan, 1970.

Viereck, Peter. *Metapolitics; The Roots of the Nazi Mind.* Rev. ed. New York: Capricorn Books, 1961.

Weber, Eugen. *Varieties of Fascism; Doctrines of Revolution in the Twentieth Century.* Princeton, N.J.: D. Van Nostrand Co., 1964.

Weiss, John. *The Fascist Tradition; Radical Right-Wing Extremism in Modern Europe.* New York: Harper & Row, 1967.

Whiteside, Andrew G. "The Nature and Origins of National Socialism." *Journal of Central European Affairs,* Vol. XVII (1957–58), pp. 48–73.

Woolf, S. J. (ed.). *The Nature of Fascism.* London: Weidenfeld and Nicolson, 1968.

6

THE IDEOLOGIES OF
THE DEVELOPING NATIONS

One of the most noteworthy changes in the post-World War II era has been the emergence of many African, Asian, and Middle Eastern countries from their colonial status. These countries represent a wide diversity of cultures and political traditions. Some, such as India, were provided with some help in preparing themselves for independence; others, such as the Congo, were given no such preparation but were thrust into independence on very short notice. Whatever their differences, these countries all face similar problems. They are generally populated with poverty-stricken, uneducated people who are not really part of the world of the 20th century but are members of traditional cultures that have resisted change for centuries. At the same time, more and more of these people are beginning to get a glimpse of the material goods available in the world today, and they want some of these goods *now*. Thus, the leaders of these countries are under various pressures to speed the rate of economic development. In addition, these people are unfamiliar with the various political and economic forms through which their countries might achieve a higher economic status. All of these points add up to a tremendous burden for the people of these new countries as they go through the process of modernization.

Political scientists are not in agreement over the exact process of modernization or the stages it involves. Part of this disagreement is because of the lack of cases of countries that have gone through the process since the industrial revolution. We also lack verifiable data on the histories of many

124

of the countries that are presently beginning the process to compare with the few completed cases we have. There are also a number of problems of a more technical nature that relate to the level of theoretical sophistication in the field of comparative politics. First, it is necessary to have a vocabulary or a set of concepts that can be easily used in a wide variety of cultures. In the past, social scientists have tended to expect the entire world to follow the pattern found in Western countries. In this way they were culture bound. Recently, social scientists have attempted to overcome this problem by developing concepts that can be applied to any culture. Second, and more difficult, it is essential to develop a theoretical framework that can explain change through time. Again, this seems to be nearing a solution but has not yet reached one.

In analyzing the ideologies found in these countries, we are faced with a number of problems in addition to the lack of agreement among social scientists. First, there is too much data. There are many countries going through the process of development and each has its own national peculiarities. Therefore, it is necessary to generalize about them, and there are usually some exceptions to any generalization.[1] Second, the ideologies involved serve a variety of purposes. They are both attempts to describe the ideal society of the future, and they are political weapons in the hands of the leaders of the country. And the mixture of these elements varies from country to country, leader to leader, and time to time. Finally, certain of the elements of these ideologies are particularly misleading. For example, with very few exceptions these countries favor "democracy" and "socialism," but very different things are meant by these terms in the various ideologies.

In order to approach this material with some system, I have organized the discussion around the following major headings—modernizing nationalism and developmental socialism. Although this approach leaves out much, these two topics are so basic that it seems justifiable to do so.

Each of the developing nations faces different problems because of their differing starting points, histories, levels of culture, economic base, literacy rate, and so on. At the same time, there are some obvious similarities, and perhaps a pattern of development is emerging. Probably the most obvious characteristic of these new nations is their nationalism.

---

[1] Some studies of individual countries and groups of countries can be found in the suggested readings at the end of the chapter.

Modernizing nationalism

Nationalism is a central concern of the developing nations because in many cases they are literally new nations with which the people have no identification. Even in those nations that are at least similar in territory and have a long-standing identification as a unit, such as India, a variety of loyalties, such as caste or language, adversely affect attempts to solve or even identify national problems. In many of the new African countries, tribal loyalties have been historically much more important than national loyalties, and in some cases tribal boundaries are not coterminous with national ones. In such cases there is a deep-rooted problem of conflicting loyalties that will cause serious difficulties for many years. The problem of conflicting loyalties connected with the desire on the part of political leaders to develop a loyalty and identification with the nation is undoubtedly one of the most serious problems for the new nations. It is clear that there is no simple solution, and it is difficult to know how to develop an identification with the nation, while not destroying the identification with tribal units, for example. This is peculiarly a problem when the tribal units cross national boundaries.

The significance of nationalism in the ideologies of the developing nations, even, or perhaps particularly, where it is not reflected in the feelings of the people, cannot be ignored. Some scholars have used the term *nation building*[2] almost as an equivalent to modernization. The point is a simple one. Can a nation exist very long and thus achieve modernization unless its citizens identify with it? How can a government solve problems unless the people view themselves as part of a unit? How do you manufacture a tradition and an identification? These questions are simple to pose, but they do not lend themselves to simple solutions. These problems are not solved with the regalia of a nation, a flag, an anthem, a great seal, an army, and so on, but all these things may help.

Japan is an interesting case of the problems and forces involved. Japan had a long tradition of rule by one family, but it had almost always actually been ruled by someone other than the emperor. In the 19th century, Japanese scholars rediscovered the historical role of the emperor as a strong ruler. This discovery, combined with a rediscovery of the traditional cul-

---

[2] See, for example, Karl W. Deutsch and William J. Foltz, eds., *Nation Building* (New York: Atherton Press, 1963).

ture, helped pave the way for a revolution to give back to the emperor the powers he had once held. The emperor was technically given back his power, but actually the tradition of dualistic rule was maintained. At the same time, the revolution helped develop a reidentification with Japan on the part of many people. The fact that this was one of the forces that ultimately led to fascism and the war in the Pacific should give one pause with regard to the development of nationalism in the new African and Asian countries.[3]

One of the major difficulties facing these nations in molding an identity is the lack of knowledge of their histories and cultures. In African countries, for example, often the histories or cultures that are known are tribal, not national, and therefore they serve as only a partial solution. These tribal cultures, some of which are highly developed and in some cases very sophisticated, were political entities in some instances. The new nations sometimes simply cut across these tribal boundaries and split up a people with an identification and included within the national boundaries people without an identification with each other or with the nation. Although some of the tribal cultures and tribal identification is of recent origin, they provide a focus of loyalty that is separate from national loyalty. This fact complicates the efforts to create a national identity and tradition.

Unfortunately for these countries, a national tradition cannot be manufactured overnight; but there is at least one factor that can be used to help develop a national identity—the colonial experience. In addition, the movement to rid the country of the colonial power usually is a nationalist movement and helps to form some identity. This does not suffice, of course, to maintain an identity after the movement has succeeded. It is clear that the colonial experience does provide some ties among the developing nations, but these ties are not deep-rooted because the colonial experiences were significantly different from country to country. The nationalist movement may also help to tie a particular nation together for awhile, but such a movement cannot last indefinitely. India is an example of a one-party dominant political system based on a nationalist movement which is today,

---

[3] In his recent book *The Ideology of Fascism; the Rationale of Totalitarianism,* A. James Gregor calls fascism ". . . the first revolutionary mass movement regime which aspired to commit the totality of human and natural resources of an historic community to national development" (New York: Free Press, 1969), p. xii. Hence the parallels between fascism and some of the recent modernization movements are probably not accidental.

about 20 years after independence, losing its political unity and having to make the adjustment to the diversty that the nationalist movement and the Congress party helped to put off for a time. Other countries will go through the same experience of having the nationalist movement hold the country together for a time, but not indefinitely.

A brief glance at the definition of nationalism advanced in Chapter 2 will illustrate the complexity of the problem. First, an individual must believe that "his own welfare and that of the significant groups to which he belongs are dependent upon the preservation or expansion (or both) of the power and culture of his society." Second, he must share a set of demands with others in his society which he believes to be justified and which incline him to personal sacrifice. The first point is the most problematic in the setting of the developing nations, but the development of a shared set of demands is almost equally difficult. Here again, we have the problem of identification with a group that simply does not exist in many of these new nations. It is problematical if such identification can be easily created. The United States was in many ways the first new nation that did succeed in developing national identity and loyalty.[4] In addition, many South American countries have seemingly succeeded in establishing some sort of identity in the minds of their people, but they are beset with all the other problems that the new nations of Africa and Asia have. Therefore, it is clear that national identity is not necessarily the solution to the problem even if one can achieve it.

The ideologies of the developing countries are designed to help form nationalism in the sense of the first point above. In addition, they constitute a set of demands that will hopefully help to weld the nation together and move it into the 20th century. When the governments cannot meet these demands, both nationalism and economic and political development fail. This point has been made before, but it should be clearly reiterated. The problems of the new nations of Africa and Asia are much greater than the problems that were faced by the new nations of North and South America, because the former are faced with an industrialized world which is able to provide many segments of the population with ease and comfort or all those things that we call affluence. The people of today's new nations get a glimpse of this affluence and want some for themselves. There-

---

[4] See Seymour M. Lipset, *First New Nation: The United States in Historical and Comparative Perspective* (New York: Basic Books, 1963).

fore, the leaders of the new nation are faced with the simultaneous problems of rapid economic development in order to provide some consumer goods, the welding of the nation into a political unit, and the development of the national identification. All of these things must somehow emerge from the chaotic situation in which any new nation finds itself. The political leaders are under tremendous pressure to produce utopia immediately. They have often promised utopia with the ending of colonialism and they cannot make it appear. Therefore, they are caught on the horns of a dilemma. They have to produce something that they cannot produce within the time given them. Therefore, all that can be expected in many of these countries for many years is turmoil, revolution, and civil war.

Obviously, for all of the new nations, the first prerequisite was or is national independence. There is a general division into two camps among the ideologies. One group contends that revolution is the only means of achieving independence; the others argue that reform or evolution is the best approach and that it is a possible approach in most, but not all, colonial areas.

The problem of revolution at the time of independence is more complicated than one might think. In the first place, a revolution can at times achieve a form of national unity; it can tie people together in a common effort and give them some sort of feeling for the country as a whole. At the same time, a revolution can be extremely destructive of whatever economic development the nation has achieved under the colonial rulers. A revolution is likely to destroy those things that the country needs immediately after independence. Therefore, in this sense, revolution is clearly a two-edged sword. It may help form national loyalties while at the same time destroying the possibility of rapid economic development or even economic independence. The evolutionary side of the argument has similar problems, but from the other angle. A gradual change toward independence has certainly seemingly immense advantages. In the first place, the colonial power may help train individuals to take over the important civil service and industrial positions that are so important for any country. The tools of economic development, the industries, the plantations and so forth, are also unlikely to be destroyed. At the same time, though, this gradual change is first and foremost gradual. It does not provide for meeting the desires of the people to be free *today*. It asks them to put off their freedom until some future date. It asks them to deny themselves this goal for a time.

It is also not as likely to produce any feeling of national unity or loyalty.

After formal independence is achieved, there is the problem of economic ties with the ex-colonial power that may constitute continuance of control. This is known as *neocolonialism*. Again, there is a revolution-evolution split in the ideologies, but most of the new countries seem able to develop some sort of rapprochement with the former colonists, usually to mutual advantage. The problem of neocolonialism is a complex one. It is clearly essential for rapid economic development that the new nation be able to trade with older, more established nations. Very often the only thing that the new nation has to trade is raw material. The colonial power most often exploited the nation by taking out its raw materials and giving little or nothing in exchange. It is hard for the leaders of the new nation to see their raw materials going to a more highly developed country, even though they are getting something in return such as manufactured goods or even industries. Therefore, many of these new nations have insisted that the processing of the raw materials they sell must take place in the country, thus producing an industry, employing people, and giving them some sense that they are not being exploited. The problem stems in large part from the fact that raw materials sell on the world market at a much lower price than do manufactured goods. Therefore, the new nation feels that it is being exploited by selling something that is relatively inexpensive in order to purchase something that is relatively expensive. They believe that they are losing.

The same thing is often true of farmers in the United States today. They argue that what they produce and are paid for sells very cheaply, but that what they have to buy in order to live is very expensive. Consequently, they feel that they are being exploited and cheated. Such attitudes make neocolonialism an extremely important and difficult issue for the new nation. It must deal with older, more developed countries, often including its previous colonial ruler, in order to survive, but it feels that it is being exploited in virtually the same way it was while it was still a colony. The difficulty of the situation is greatly enhanced when the former colonial power is one of the neocolonial powers because there are certain identifications in the mind of the people and particularly in the nationalist leaders that make it very difficult for them to view the old rulers objectively and deal with them solely in economic terms. Still, some sort of arrangement is necessary which will provide each side with the economic goods that they require while avoiding this neocolonialist label. This problem has not been solved as yet.

A third part of contemporary nationalism has been noted already, the attempt to develop or revive an indigenous culture.[5] Julius Nyerere, first president of Tanzania, put it this way in his inaugural address:

> The major change I have made is to get up an entirely new Ministry: the Ministry of National Culture and Youth. I have done this because I believe that its culture is the essence and spirit of any nation. A country which lacks its own culture is no more than a collection of people without the spirit which makes them a nation. Of all the crimes of colonialism there is none worse than the attempt to make us believe we had no indigenous culture of our own; or that what we did have was worthless—something of which we should be ashamed, instead of a source of pride.[6]

This attempt to revitalize indigenous cultures is characteristic of most of the new nations, but it can pose serious problems when certain traditions or aspects of the culture impede development. In India, for example, caste works against cooperation across caste lines, religious proscriptions stand in the way of an adequate diet, and language differences fragment the society as a whole. Thus, a concern for culture and tradition can both help and impede the process of modernization. We do not know enough about the particular traditional cultures of Africa to be able to say much about the extent to which these cultures impede or help industrialization. It has been contended that the religious system of Puritanism helped greatly in the development of capitalism and hence industrialization in the United States.[7] Likewise, there may be elements of the religious systems of Africa and Asia that will either help or impede industrialization. We simply do not as yet know enough about the situations to say.

Two other patterns, both in the process of change, need to be mentioned: regionalism and nonalignment. The developing countries have, with the exception of the Latin American countries, who may not be

---

[5] Black Nationalism in the United States is faced with a similar problem—how to develop a black culture as a basis for the nationalist movement.

[6] Julius K. Nyerere, "President's Inaugural Address," in *Freedom and Unity: A Selection from Writings and Speeches 1952–65* (Nairobi: Oxford University Press, 1966), p. 186. Reprinted by permission of President Nyerere and Oxford University Press.

[7] See Max Weber, *The Protestant Ethic and the Spirit of Capitalism*, trans., Talcott Parsons (New York: Charles Scribner's Sons, 1930).

free to choose, attempted to avoid aligning themselves with any side in the various disagreements among the major powers of the world. And the Latin American countries are beginning to follow this pattern. At the same time, they have attempted to form regional coalitions to help solve common problems and to present a united front to the world. Regionalism, though, is of growing importance. Although the attempts to join two or more countries together have generally failed, loose regional coalitions have provided a forum for the consideration of common problems and has led to some cooperation.

But regionalism will not develop into confederation or federation as long as the dominant theme in the ideologies is nationalism. Nonalignment also serves the nationalistic aspects of the ideologies. It seems likely that nationalism will remain the key element and that it will continue to be encouraged as a means of unifying the people of the developing nations.

Developmental socialism[8]

The overwhelming majority of the new nations label themselves "socialist," but they mean a wide variety of things by the word. Perhaps the only area in which complete agreement is found is in the rejection of capitalism, but even here there is a problem. The capitalism they are rejecting is the traditional, completely laissez-faire capitalism that no longer exists in the world today. But the rejecting of capitalism, which leads to labeling diverse economic systems as *socialism,* is an important phenomenon whether or not capitalism is accurately perceived. The underlying reason for the antipathy to capitalism lies in the identification of capitalism with colonialism and neocolonialism. There is sufficient justification for such identification to develop a deep-rooted fear and rejection of the label *capitalism,* whatever the actual economic system may be. In addition, this rejection of capitalism should be more thoroughly related to the problem of nationalism in the developing countries. We have said that one of the reasons for the rejection of capitalism is the underlying rejection of the colonial system which was based on capitalism. Therefore, the result of this is simply that, given the major economic systems available in the world today, the developing nations are most likely to accept socialism be-

---

[8] This section owes much to Chapter 10, "Socialism as a Program for Development," in Charles W. Anderson, Fred R. von der Mehden, and Crawford Young, *Issues of Political Development* (Englewood Cliffs, N.J.: Prentice-Hall, 1967), pp. 175–219.

cause it can be seen as part of nationalism in the context of their particular situations.

Anderson, von der Mehden, and Young have suggested a typology of contemporary developmental socialism that is extremely useful.[9] They argue that the various socialisms found in the developing nations may be reduced to five:

1. Doctrinaire Marxist-Leninist socialism
2. Radical, Mobilization socialism
3. Eclectic socialism based on peasant revolution
4. Communitarian socialism
5. Moderate Reformist socialism

Of these five types of socialism, Radical, Mobilization socialism and Moderate Reformist socialism are the most common, according to their analyses.

Since we have already discussed Marxism, there is no point in reiterating what has already been said. Although Doctrinaire Marxist-Leninist socialism has not been very popular among the developing countries, it is interesting in other respects. Only the developing Communist countries, such as China, North Vietnam, North Korea, and Cuba have adopted this approach. In the other countries, it is represented by Communist political parties or other groups, such as national liberation movements, that are attempting to gain political power—so far they have been unsuccessful. This lack of success has a variety of causes, and assigning specific causes to specific cases would be foolhardy without a detailed analysis of all the factors involved, but it seems clear that one of the major reasons is the rejection of the Marxist-Leninist approach by most of the leaders of the developing nations.

The major point of interest in modern Marxist-Leninist socialism is found in the way it is being taken seriously by Western revolutionaries. Three men in particular, Mao Tse-tung, Ho Chi Minh, and Ernesto Che Guevara, are honored by Western revolutionaries. The three are symbols of the struggle against capitalism and Western imperialism and neo-colonialism, and they are very important in this sense. Except for Mao's contributions to the theory of the revolution through guerilla warfare that we noted in Chapter 3, they have made few, if any, significant contributions to communism.

---

[9] Ibid., pp. 190–92.

Although only Mao is an orthodox Marxist, both Ho and Che tended to theorize within Marxist thought, but that is not their importance. Ho was a Vietnamese nationalist who successfully fought the West. "He has been too much the doer, the organizer, the conspirator, and, finally, the father of his own country to engage in the contemplation that serious writing generally requires."[10]

Che was the perfect archetype of the modern revolutionary. He was deeply concerned with the poverty he found all over Central and South America, and he fought to improve things. And whatever his motivation may have been, when one revolution was successfully completed, he joined another where he was killed. Young, intelligent, a fighter and a martyr—there could be no better combination to impress young revolutionaries around the world.

Both Ho and Che are important symbols of nationalism and revolution. Mao is also a symbol in these senses, but in addition he leads a successful developing country—the most populous in the world. Therefore, even though the leaders of the developing nations are not Communist, they view China and Mao with considerable interest. The leaders of the developing nations are concerned with success more than form, and they hope to draw lessons from Mao.

Mao's importance is not due primarily to communism, but to the success achieved in:

1. Winning a revolution
2. Consolidating this revolution over a vast area and population
3. Managing to feed this vast population better than previous regimes
4. Beginning, with many setbacks, to industrialize

Since these are the goals of both hopeful and successful revolutionary leaders, Mao is listened to. But, since there is little evidence that communism was an essential ingredient in Mao's achievements, they do not always listen to that part of his message. They are more concerned with the techniques of mobilizing the population.

Radical, Mobilization socialism is primarily concerned, as its title indicates, with developing methods of mobilizing the population in support of

---

[10] Bernard B. Fall, "Ho Chi Minh—A Profile," in Fall, ed., *Ho Chi Minh on Revolution; Selected Writings, 1920–66* (New York: New American Library, 1967), p. v.

rapid economic development. This mobilization is usually carried out under the direction of a single political party and requires complete state control of the economy. It tends to be highly nationalistic and therefore rejects ties that would make it dependent on any developed country. Although there are many fewer such systems now than there were just a few years ago, it is the dominant pattern. The arguments in favor of such a system are based on the belief that an authoritarian government that is able to act quickly and efficiently is essential for the rapid economic development of the country. The arguments against the system vary from the obvious corruption found under rulers such as Nkrumah to the contention by some radicals that it gives power to the conservatives. It is commonly assumed that such a system may well be necessary immediately after independence but that it will have to be changed within a few years.

Beyond this tendency, it is difficult to see a pattern within the single parties themselves. None of them, with the exception of the Communist regimes, can be called totalitarian. Moderates as well as radicals are capable of corruption. Some successes should also be noted—in some countries the single parties have avoided corruption and succeeded in welding together their diverse populations into a nation. It is important not to be overly optimistic. It is too soon to tell if these countries have been successful enough to develop a national identity in the long run.

Often the alternative to single-party rule has been military rule. The usual result has been rule by force and fear and a loss of contact with, and sensitivity to, the people. The result has generally been a return to civilian rule. During the period of military rule, the only general pattern that emerges, with Ghana as a partial exception, is the continuance of a single dominant ruler. But usually, Nasser being an exception, this occurs without a charismatic leader who can gain the support of the people. Nasser was also an exception in realizing that political parties would be necessary to feel out public opinion. The sharp division and lack of communication between the people and the military rulers are the major reasons for their collapse.

Eclectic socialism based on peasant revolution "is distinguished by the fact of a successful revolution, based largely on the rural lower class, which definitely reshaped the structure of power in the society. . . ."[11] Algeria

---

[11] Anderson, von der Mehden, and Young, *Issues of Political Development*, p. 191.

and Bolivia followed this pattern. At various points in its history, Mexico also has followed this pattern. The result is usually to emphasize agrarian reform and economic nationalism. This approach to socialism is not particularly important in the new nations of Africa and Asia, particularly Africa, because the agricultural patterns do not seem to produce the same type of peasant class that we find in Europe and parts of Asia. At least this class has not been molded into a revolutionary movement as it was in Algeria and China, but the major point of Eclectic socialism is that the reform is primarily land reform centering on a redistribution of land to the peasantry either individually or collectively. This type of reform does not lend itself to industrialization and modernization if it stops there. The redistribution of land is likely, at least for a time, to result in higher production of agricultural goods, but an industrializing society needs to gradually take people off the land and move them into urban areas as laborers in industries rather than as peasants. Thus, Eclectic socialism has a basic difficulty built into its very form.

Communitarian socialism stresses a harmonious social order. It is similar in many ways to the communitarianism found in the United States in the 19th century, although the U.S. example stressed withdrawn communities. The emphasis is on social solidarity and cooperation. Examples of leaders representing this approach are Leopold Senghor (Senegal), Julius Nyerere (Tanzania), U Nu (Burma), and Vinoba Bhave (India). Communitarian socialism is a form of socialism which stresses a close-knit relationship among the individuals within the society. Normally, in Communitarian socialism the land and all other economic goods are owned and controlled by the society as a whole. Distribution in such a society is usually based on need, although at times it is based on labor performed. There is often a religious basis to the Communitarian socialist approach, both in the historical examples in the United States and in the contemporary examples in Asia and Africa. The religion helps to provide a tie among the people which then can be developed into an identification with the community. Thus, Communitarian socialism has built into it the means of developing national identity.

Moderate Reformist socialism resembles a dumping ground for what is left over, but a careful analysis of the groups involved reveals some basic similarities. Development is seen as gradual and usually democratically controlled. The major emphasis is on governmental regulation of a predominately private economy.[12] Moderate Reformist socialism is essentially little different from contemporary capitalism. The difference is primarily that of a label that is popular among developing nations.

With the exception of the Communist countries, all of these brands of socialism have allowed some degree of private ownership. They are more concerned with rapid development than with ideological niceties. Therefore, *socialism* in this sense must not be simply defined as if it were the same thing as traditional socialism. Developmental socialism is oriented toward rapid economic development, nationalism, and the integration of new societies. It is not primarily a doctrine of governmental control of the economy. The focus of developmental socialism is contained in the word *developmental*. The whole thrust of this approach is to get the country going, to move from a fairly primitive form of economy into the modern world, with abundant consumers goods and affluence the goals. Developmental socialism is fundamentally materialistic in this sense, but it is also closely connected with nationalism. These nations cannot exist unless they are able to develop economically and move themselves into the 20th century. They cannot do this without rapid industrialization. It is their belief that by having the government play a strong role in the economy, ranging from complete dominance to regulation, the nation will be able to mobilize its economic resources in such a way as to bring about this rapid industrialization. They also believe that, by having the government do this, it will be easier to weld the nation into a unit than if individual entrepreneurs controlled the economy.

Suggested readings

Almond, Gabriel A., and Powell, G. Bingham. *Comparative Politics; A Developmental Approach.* Boston: Little, Brown & Co., 1966.

Anderson, Charles W.; von der Mehden, Fred R.; and Young, Crawford. *Issues of Political Development.* Englewood Cliffs, N.J.: Prentice-Hall, 1967.

Apter, David. *Ghana in Transition.* Rev. ed. New York: Atheneum, 1963.

————. *The Political Kingdom in Uganda: A Study in Bureaucratic Nationalism.* Princeton, N.J.: Princeton University Press, 1961.

————. *The Politics of Modernization.* Chicago: University of Chicago Press, 1965.

---

[12] Ibid., p. 192.

Binder, Leonard. *Iran: Political Development in a Changing Society*. Berkeley: University of California Press, 1962.

Black, Cyrile. *The Dynamics of Modernization*. New York: Harper & Row, 1966.

Brecher, Michael. *The New States of Asia; A Political Analysis*. New York: Oxford University Press, 1963.

Brockway, Fenner. *African Socialism; A Background Book*. Chester Springs, Pa.: Dufour Editions, 1963.

Burnett, Ben G., and Kenneth F. Johnson. *Political Forces in Latin America: Dimensions of the Quest for Stability*. 2nd ed. Belmont, Calif.: Wadsworth Publishing Co., 1970.

Coleman, James S. *The Politics of Developing Areas*. Princeton, N.J.: Princeton University Press, 1960.

———. (ed.). *Education and Political Development*. Princeton, N.J.: Princeton University Press, 1965.

Deutsch, Karl W., and Foltz, William J. (eds.). *Nation Building*. New York: Atherton Press, 1963.

Eisenstadt, S. N. *The Political Systems of Empires*. New York: Free Press, 1963.

Fall, Bernard B. (ed.). *Ho Chi Minh On Revolution; Selected Writings, 1920–66*. New York: New American Library, 1967.

Fickett, Lewis, Jr. *Problems of the Developing Nations: Readings and Case Studies*. New York: Thomas Y. Crowell Co., 1966.

Friedland, William H., and Rosberg, Carl G. (eds.). *African Socialism*. Stanford, Calif.: Stanford University Press, 1964.

Geertz, Clifford (ed.). *Old Societies and New States: Quest for Modernity in Asia and Africa*. New York: The Free Press, 1963.

Gerassi, John (ed.). *Venceremos! The Speeches and Writings of Ernesto Che Guevara*. New York: Simon and Schuster, 1968.

Guevara, Ernesto Che. *Reminiscenses of the Cuban Revolutionary War*. Trans. Victoria Ortiz. New York: Monthly Review Press, 1968.

———. *Socialism and Man*. New York: Young Socialist Alliance, 1969.

Holt, Robert T., and Turner, John E. *The Political Basis of Economic Development: An Exploration in Comparative Political Analysis*. Princeton, N.J.: D. Van Nostrand Co., 1966.

Horowitz, Irving Louis. *Three Worlds of Development: The Theory and Practice of International Stratification*. New York: Oxford University Press, 1966.

———; De Castro, Josué; and Gerassi, John (eds.). *Latin American Radicalism: A Documentary Report on Left and Nationalist Movements*. New York: Random House, 1969.

Janowitz, Morris. *The Military in the Political Development of New Nations.* Chicago: University of Chicago Press, 1964.

Kautsky, John H. (ed.). *Political Change in Underdeveloped Countries: Nationalism and Communism.* New York: John Wiley & Sons, 1962.

Kebschull, Harvey G. (ed.). *Politics in Transitional Societies; The Challenge of Change in Asia, Africa, and Latin America.* New York: Appleton-Century-Crofts, 1968.

La Palombara, Joseph (ed.). *Bureaucracy and Political Development.* Princeton, N.J.: Princeton University Press, 1963.

Legum, Colin. *Pan-Africanism.* New York: Frederick A. Praeger, 1965.

Lerner, Daniel. *The Passing of Traditional Societies; Modernizing the Middle East.* New York: The Free Press, 1958.

Levy, Marion J., Jr. *Modernization and the Structure of Society.* 2 vols. Princeton, N.J.: Princeton University Press, 1966.

Markovitz, Irving Leonard (ed.). *African Politics and Society; Basic Issues and Problems of Government and Development.* New York: The Free Press, 1970.

Miller, J. D. B. *The Politics of the Third World.* London: Oxford University Press, 1966.

Millikan, Max F., and Blackmer, Donald L. (eds.). *The Emerging Nations: Their Growth and United States Policy.* Boston: Little Brown & Co., 1961.

Millikan, Max F., and Hapgood, David. *No Easy Harvest; The Dilemma of Agriculture in Underdeveloped Countries.* Boston: Little, Brown and Co., 1967.

Montgomery, John D., and Siffin, William J. (eds.). *Approaches to Development: Politics, Administration and Change.* New York: McGraw-Hill Book Co., 1966.

Nyerere, Julius K. *Freedom and Socialism; A Selection from Writings and Speeches 1965–1970.* Dar es Salaam: Oxford University Press, 1968.

———. *Freedom and Unity; A Selection from Writings and Speeches 1952–67.* Nairobi: Oxford University Press, 1966.

Organski, A. F. K. *The Stages of Political Development.* New York: Alfred A. Knopf, 1965.

Pye, Lucian. *Aspects of Political Development.* Boston: Little, Brown & Co., 1966.

———. *Politics, Personality and Nation Building. Burma's Search for Identity.* New Haven, Conn.: Yale University Press, 1962.

——— (ed.). *Communications and Political Development.* Princeton, N.J.: Princeton University Press, 1963.

———, and Verba, Sidney. *Political Culture and Political Development.* Princeton, N.J.: Princeton University Press, 1966.

Riggs, Fred W. *Administration in Developing Countries: The Theory of Prismatic Society.* Boston: Houghton Mifflin Co., 1964.

———. *Thailand: The Modernization of a Bureaucratic Polity.* Honolulu: East-West Center Press, 1966.

Sayegh, Fayez A. (ed.). *The Dynamics of Neutralism in the Arab World: A Symposium.* San Francisco: Chandler Publishing Co., 1964.

Schapera, I. *Government and Politics in Tribal Society.* New York: Frederick A. Praeger, 1964.

Senghor, Leopold Sedar. *On African Socialism.* New York: Frederick A. Praeger, 1964.

Shaffer, Harry G., and Prybyla, Jan S. (eds.). *From Underdevelopment to Affluence; Western, Soviet, and Chinese Views.* New York: Appleton-Century-Crofts, 1968.

Shils, Edward. *Political Development in the New States.* The Hague: Mouton, 1962.

Sigmund, Paul E. (ed.). *The Ideologies of the Developing Nations.* New York: Frederick A. Praeger, 1967.

Von der Mehden, Fred R., *Politics of the Developing Nations.* 2nd ed. Englewood Cliffs, N.J.: Prentice-Hall, 1969.

Von Vorys, Karl. *Political Development in Pakistan.* Princeton, N.J.: Princeton University Press, 1965.

Ward, Robert E., and Rustow, Dankwart A. *Political Modernization in Japan and Turkey.* Princeton, N.J.: Princeton University Press, 1964.

Wriggins, W. Howard. *Ceylon: Dilemmas of a New Nation.* Princeton, N.J.: Princeton University Press, 1960.

Zeitlin, Maurice. *Revolutionary Politics and the Cuban Working Class.* New York: Harper & Row, 1970.

7

THE NEW LEFT[1]

The New Left is a rapidly changing phenomenon of the past decade. The term was first used by a group of liberal Marxists centered around the *New Left Review* in 1959. The term was then appropriated by the growing world student movement and the mass media in the mid-60s.[2] It is now used to cover a wide variety of movements and individuals, primarily in the United States but with connections to similar movements around the world.[3]

There are three reasonable approaches to a study of the New Left. One could do a study of the history of the movement, an analysis of the organizations now involved in the movement, or an analysis of the ideas that tie the movement together. I have chosen to take the third approach for three reasons. In the first place, I find it more enjoyable. In the second place, the other two approaches have distinct disadvantages, the primary one being that both analyses would be immediately out of date. Thirdly, it is my contention that the ideas are the defining characteristics of the New Left and that the movement cannot be understood from any other perspective.

---

[1] For a more extensive and detailed analysis of New Left thought, see my forthcoming book, *The Social and Political Thought of the New Left: An Introduction*, to be published by the Dorsey Press.

[2] For chronologies of the movement, see Julian Nagel, ed., *Student Power* (London: Merlin Press, 1969), pp. 225–35, and Massimo Teodori, ed., *The New Left: A Documentary History* (Indianapolis, Ind.: Bobbs-Merrill, 1969), pp. 447–82.

[3] For studies of these movements see, for example, Barbara Ehrenreich and John E. Ehrenreich, *Long March, Short Spring; The Student Uprising at Home and Abroad* (New York: Monthly Review Press, 1969).

It should be noted that two movements separate from but linked to the New Left, the black movement and the women's movement, can be included in most but not all of the points made below. Among the groups that compose the movement, including the black groups and the women's groups, there are widely divergent emphases, but all agree on the goals I set forth with the exception of the purely reformist groups. All the radical groups clearly agree on these points. The major disagreements on the New Left are over tactics and to discuss these points in detail is beyond the scope of this chapter. It should be kept in mind, therefore, that the focus is on the general agreements, and it should be remembered that disagreements are plentiful.

In looking at the New Left we shall look first at the New Left's criticism of contemporary society and then at the New Left's values and goals. Finally, we shall look at the New Left utopia by way of conclusion.

Criticism of contemporary society

Throughout most of its life the New Left has been most noted for its critical stance toward contemporary society rather than its goals. In order to understand fully the impact and the importance of the New Left we must note its attack on contemporary Western culture.

The most basic criticism is hypocrisy—the divergence between word and deed. This point is not monopolized by the New Left; it is widely believed that the expressed values of Western society must not be deeply felt because so few attempts seem to be made to actually practice them.

In addition to this basic criticism, there are so many points of attack that I shall simply list them in brief notes.

I. The Political System
   A. Insufficient means included in representative democracy for the people to be involved in the decision-making process
   B. Corruption
   C. Resistance to significant change
   D. Political repression
II. The Economic System
   A. Poverty alongside great wealth
   B. Emphasis on unnecessary consumer goods rather than socially beneficial production

C. Centralization of economic power—monopoly capitalism

D. Lack of concern with side effects of the industrial process, such as pollution

E. Economic imperialism (neocolonialism)—exploitation of developing nations

III. Racism and Sexism

Discrimination against minority groups and women in all aspects of life.

IV. Socialization System

A. Education

1. Lack of "relevance"

2. Authoritarian atmosphere

3. Expresses the bad aspects of the rest of the social system

B. Religion

1. Not "relevant"

2. Tied to capitalist system

3. Particular target of charge of hypocrisy

C. Family

1. Marriage an institution of private property

2. Marriage should not need religious and/or legal approval

3. Hypocrisy about sex—sexual repression

4. Poor way to raise children

The basic values and goals

It is possible to analyze the New Left through a series of values and goals that seem to be found among all the groups and individuals that make up the movement. These are:

1. The emphasis on action
2. The search for the authentic self
3. Community
4. Equality
5. Liberty
6. Participatory democracy
7. Revolution

We will look at each of these in turn.

Action. Probably the most basic assumption of the New Left, drawn in large part from the French existentialists,[4] is that action is more important than thought. This means (1) that the individual defines himself and his values through his deeds rather than his words; (2) that change cannot or will not be brought about by the pen; and (3) that there is a degree of distrust and dislike of the intellectual on the New Left. This principle incorporates, more for the New Left than it did for the existentialists, a basic anti-intellectualism. This anti-intellectualism, in addition to being an American tradition, also relates to the basic criticism of Western society—hypocrisy. The divergence between expressed values and the actions based on these values coupled with a predilection for action tends toward an emphasis on the immediate, spontaneous act and a disparagement of reasoned discourse.

Since it is exceedingly difficult to express feelings precisely in words, the New Left has searched for other means of communication. The art forms of the 60s, happenings, the environments directed at one or a combination of the senses, are attempts to get beyond the verbal to a more total communication. Earlier, in the 50s, poets such as Allen Ginsberg tried to shake and jolt people out of their lethargy and their preconceptions. With obscenities and with the language molded to meet new thought patterns, these writers were beginning to do the same thing that later shifted from the verbal and became the happenings. The same point can be made about the music. Although the words often express the sentiments of the New Left, they are much less important than the total environment produced by the sound.[5]

The authentic self. Although most intellectuals disparage the short movement called the beatniks, they are important for understanding the development of New Left thought. In the first place, a number of individuals, such as Ginsberg and Gary Snyder, figure prominently in both

---

[4] The intellectual origins of the New Left have not been adequately explored. The existentialists, particularly Albert Camus, expressed positions remarkably similar to those now expressed by the New Left. It is likely that influence is demonstrable, but such a task cannot be undertaken here. The interested reader should consult the works of Camus; William Barrett, *Irrational Man; A Study in Existential Philosophy* (Garden City, N.Y.: Doubleday Anchor Books, 1958); and Michel Antoine Burnier, *Choice of Action; The French Existentialists on the Political Front Line,* trans., Bernard Murchland (New York: Random House, 1968).

[5] For a general discussion of the relationship between the New Left and art, see Donald Drew Egbert, *Social Radicalism and the Arts; Western Europe* (New York: Alfred A. Knopf, 1970), pp. 359–64, 571–80, and passim.

cultures. Secondly, the criticisms of contemporary society are strikingly similar. Thirdly, the basic motivation of the beats (coming from the word *beatific*) was the same as a strong current now found on the New Left— a desparate search for something authentic, something solid in the self. Clearly this was transmitted from the existentialists, but it was transmitted through the beat subculture.

Probably the greatest difference between the beats and the New Left is that the New Left has some hope of finding something. The beats were called the product of the age of apathy—they were in reality the generation of despair. The primary beat novels, *On the Road* (1957) and *The Dharma Bums* (1958) by Jack Kerouac, are pervaded by a sense of despair periodically broken by a glory in being alive.

The New Left is still searching for this authentic self, and it seems to have some hope of finding it in notions of community, the group, and, of course, action. Often the last idea is expressed in the concept of revolution. Hence a number of the basic goals and values of the New Left are tied together with the search for the authentic self.[6] This is particularly true of the concept of community.

Community. Notions of community or group consciousness are not common or particularly popular in American political thought, but they form the central concept in New Left thought. The basic idea is most often associated with the hippie communes, but it is a pervasive motif of the New Left. The revolutionary moves from communal apartment to communal apartment; the typical hippie lives in a rural or urban community withdrawn from the surrounding straight world.[7]

Whatever specific form it takes, the social organization most favored by the New Left is community or group based rather than based on the individual. The New Left is suggesting the development of many fairly small face-to-face highly interactive groups. Two novels express this idea —Robert A. Heinlein's *Stranger in a Strange Land* (1961) and Robert Rimmer's *Harrad Experiment* (1966). Both present the basic ideas of the New Left notion of community:

---

[6] This may account for the popularity of the novels of Herman Hesse, particularly *Magister Ludi*, also called *The Bead Game* and *Das Glasperlenspiel* (1943), which presents a search for an undefined goal certainly related to the self through both individual and community effort.

[7] See Gary Snyder, "Why Tribe," in *Earth House Hold*, reprinted in Harold Jaffe and John Tytell, eds., *The American Experience; A Radical Reader* (New York: Harper & Row, 1970), pp. 258–61.

1. All essentials shared
2. Deep interpersonal relations with many or all members of the group
3. Recognition of individual needs and differences

A fourth point that these novels include that a substantial part of the New Left accepts is group or shared sex.

The most important of these concepts is the first. This is the expression of a true communalism comparable to the widespread communal movement of the 19th century. It goes well beyond the fairly simple idea of sharing money. It is much more comparable to the sort of sharing that goes on within the family. Money, food, clothing, shelter, and all other necessities and luxuries are available, if possible, for the taking. It is assumed that as in a family no one will bankrupt the group or cheat the group. This assumption is possible because of the mutually supportive atmosphere produced by point two above. Each individual is emotionally tied to many or all of the others. This love is not exclusive. It does not focus on one sex-love partner but is shared with others. The practice is varied. Monogamous heterosexual relationships are very common in the New Left communes, but so are a number of other types—heterosexual, homosexual or lesbian, and bisexual. It is only fair to say that group or shared sex is widespread and growing. The basic principle involved is simply that the character of such relationships must be based on free choice. Here we note the relationship of point three above to the others, and we will return to it in discussing liberty below.

To summarize, then, the community or group is the basis of New Left thought. It presupposes close interpersonal relations among a small number of free and equal individuals. The hippie commune is the best known form of the community. The commune fulfills a variety of functions in the counterculture of the New Left. Most importantly it provides an arena in which the new life styles may be practiced with relatively little interference from the outside world. And the experience of the communes and of similar movements in the 19th century indicate that the outside world is usually ready to interfere.[8]

---

[8] Many of the communes have experienced harassment by the citizenry and police of the surrounding area. The most nearly comparable community of the 19th century, the Oneida Community, which practiced a system of "complex marriage" in which all members were considered to be married to all other members, was often harassed by the people of the area.

Related to its function of providing an arena for practicing the new life styles, the communes sometimes provide a resting area for the activists of the New Left. In this sense they are analogous to, if not strictly comparable to, the resting area that is so basic to guerrilla warfare. The guerrilla, whether urban or rural, needs a place to rest and recover between sorties. In some cases the communes provide this service.

Finally, the commune system is the model of the future society. This society will be composed of a series of interrelated communes with each one being fairly free and independent. We will return to this point after we have looked at the other basic goals of the New Left.[9]

Equality. Since in the United States the New Left developed out of the civil rights movement, it is not surprising that considerations of equality have provided a significant area of concern in New Left thought. The New Left is traditionally democratic in its concern with political and legal equality, and these notions are reflections of the civil rights movement and its concern with reforming the system.

The New Left views economic equality as a singularly important mechanism for bringing about political and legal equality. The New Left is becoming more and more socialist in its orientation with the traditional democratic socialist concern with greatly diminishing the degree of economic inequality within society. The New Left has on the whole been unexceptional in its comments on economic questions and so has contributed little except vague comments about socialism.

Probably the most interesting of the New Left's developments in the area of equality has been in the area of social equality. There seems to be two points involved here. First, there is the more or less traditional notion of equality—that individuals are to be treated the same in certain specifiable areas. The second, and much more interesting point, is that difference is to be recognized. The argument is a little difficult to specify, but it seems to focus on (1) a rejection of the notion that most differences are unimportant, (2) an assertion that certain differences have positive value, and (3) the contention that individuals must be accorded the same rights within society.

---

[9] A number of journals have sprung up to deal with the communes. *The Whole Earth Catalog* was the prototype for a large number of shopping guides and information centers. *The Modern Utopian* in the United States and *Communes* in England act as media of communications among and about the communes.

The importance of this conception of equality can be found in two areas. First, it is a departure from most democratic theory that asserts that differences are fairly unimportant. Second, it rejects the general practice that certain differences, such as sex and race, bring inferior status. The differences are seen as positive rather than negative, but it is stressed that treatment of individuals should be the same.[10]

The relationship of this conception of equality to the idea of community should be fairly clear. First, groups that assert their difference provide one basis for the formation of community life. In this way, there might develop a community drawn from the black movement or some other group that has an established group identity. Second, within the community, individuals are treated equally. Each person shares the goods of the community as he or she needs them. They contribute on the same basis; as goods are acquired that are needed by the community, they are donated to the community.

Liberty. This is to be seen in conjunction with an emphasis on individual freedom. There is no compulsion to participate in the community. If an individual does not find the mores of one community congenial, he can try to find another that is more suitable.

The New Left is noted for slogans such as "Do your own thing," and one finds that the notion of liberty is important to the New Left. First, there is the general point that contemporary culture is considered too restrictive. Therefore, the New Left wants to remove the restrictions. Second, there is the assertion that everyone must be accorded certain basic economic rights. Again, this is seen primarily as a criticism of contemporary society's failure to provide the necessities of life to everyone. The New Left contends that society must be restructured to insure that everyone has food, clothing, shelter, and whatever else is essential to life. Third, each person must in addition then be free to find and express his own personality in his own way. This entails the traditional democratic rights of free speech, assembly, press, and so forth.

It can of course be contended that members of the New Left do not

---

[10] For basic material on this topic, see Francis L. Broderick and August Meier, eds., *Negro Protest Thought in the Twentieth Century* (Indianapolis, Ind.: Bobbs-Merrill, 1965); Richard P. Young, ed., *Roots of Rebellion; The Evolution of Black Politics and Protest Since World War II* (New York: Harper & Row, 1970); and Robin Morgan, ed., *Sisterhood Is Powerful; An Anthology of Writings from the Women's Liberation Movement* (New York: Random House, 1970).

always allow others the exercise of these freedoms. They do attempt to stop, and sometimes succeed in stopping, their opponents from speaking. To some extent this may be seen as a tactical question, but that hides a deeper point. Some believe that any means are appropriate to bring about the goals, but the main point is that the opponent (1) excludes the New Left from a fair hearing from its manipulation of the media; and (2) is so conditioned by contemporary society that it cannot give the New Left a fair hearing. Therefore, (1) stopping speakers is simply using the tactics of the enemy, and (2) it is a device that may shock the opponent into examining his position.

In addition to free speech, and so on, the freedom to find and express one's authentic self means the ability to experiment with a variety of life styles, which in turn entails the freedom to do anything that does not harm another. One may harm one's self in any way he wishes. The only limit is harming another. This limit is obviously modified during a revolution.

Finally, the individual and society are seen as freeing themselves from a dependence on material goods. There is an ethos of voluntary poverty on the New Left. This is true first to identify with the oppressed masses, but second, and more importantly, it is a step toward freeing society from the oppression of consumerism.

Participatory democracy. It appears that participatory democracy is a device by which direct democracy might be feasible within a large society. Essentially participatory democracy suggests that, instead of having a large representative body, the decision-making structure be significantly altered so that there would be many small decision-making bodies throughout any given area. There have been very few statements about the level of government or administration above this small local unit. Thus there seems to be little thought of mechanisms for overcoming the probably inevitable conflict between groups who perceive the effect on their lives of a particular decision to be significantly different. Thus there seems to be no way of reconciling the interests of two groups who differ on a particular question. There is some notion that power should reside with those who are most directly affected by a particular decision, but the objections to this are so obvious that it cannot be thought of without major revision and refinement. In this context it may be worthwhile to state the most obvious of these objections—the impossibility in most cases of measuring direct effect.

On the other hand, although participatory democracy is vague, we must not ignore the role it plays in New Left thought. Participatory democracy is the logical extension of the ideas of community and social equality mentioned above. No matter which notion came first in time, participatory democracy would only be possible if the other two conditions were met. Whether or not it would be possible even under those conditions is another problem.

Revolution. The New Left believes that it will take a revolution to change contemporary Western society. At one time the revolution was to be peaceful and nonviolent and take place through gradual reform. More and more it is to be violent and bloody. The change is due to two main factors—frustration and the idealization of the guerrilla fighter. Clearly frustration is the primary reason, but if the guerrilla fighter images of Mao, Ho, and particularly Che were not available the frustration might have taken different directions.

The New Left is frustrated by the unwillingness of Western society to respond positively to its criticism, criticism that is so obviously correct. Hence, the shift began to take place to a belief that Western society has gone so far it cannot be reformed from within but must be toppled and a new, better society built in its place.

The revolution plays a peculiar role in New Left thought. First, it is a necessary step before the new society can come about. Second, it is seen as taking place over a long period of time, and it has already begun. Therefore, some members of the New Left today consider themselves to be active revolutionaries. And the revolution justifies all. Society is so corrupt that it must be changed root and branch before a good society will be possible.

The New Left is split on this point. Many favor violent revolution. Many still believe in the efficacy of nonviolence. But all want the revolution.

The New Left utopia

In a brief summary let us try to construct a model of the future society envisioned by the New Left—its utopia. Since a full description of the future society would be overly repetitious and would consume too much space, I shall simply outline it.

Political System
Participatory democracy—town meeting or direct democracy made possible by the reorganization of society into small communities. Government primarily concerned with the administration of the economic system and insuring that each individual has the basic necessities of life.
Economic System
Public ownership of all large industries, transportation, and so forth. Distribution on the basis of need wherever possible. Restructuring of the economic system to reduce the production of inessentials. Heavy reliance on automation combined with a growth of craft industries.
Social Stratification and mobility systems—nonexistent
Socialization System
Family
Marriage and sexual relations based on free choice without need of religious and/or legal sanction.
Children raised by the community
Education
Material taught determined by students and teachers in free and equal consultation
All work desired to be made available
Religion—based on free choice

These are the basic characteristics of the future society of the New Left. Many details have been left out, but the important characteristics have been noted. As with any utopia, it is likely to be changed in practice.

Suggested readings

Since there are not yet any good bibliographies available on the New Left, I have included here a much longer bibliography than I have for any other chapter.

Aaron, Daniel, et al. "Confrontation: The Old Left and the New." *The American Scholar,* Vol. XXXVI (Autumn, 1967), pp. 567–88. The entire issue is valuable.

Anderson, Albert T., and Biggs, Bernice Prince (eds.). *A Focus on Rebellion.* San Francisco: Chandler Publishing Co., 1962.

Anderson, Walt (ed.). *The Age of Protest.* Pacific Palisades, Calif.: Goodyear Publishing Co., 1969.

Aron, Raymond. *The Elusive Revolution; Anatomy of a Student Revolt.* London: Pall Mall Press, 1969.

Aronson, Ronald, and Cowley, John L. "The New Left in the United States." In *The Socialist Register 1967.* Eds. Ralph Miliband and John Savile. New York: Monthly Review Press, 1967, pp. 73–90.

Aya, Roderick, and Miller, Norman (eds.). *The New American Revolution.* New York: The Free Press, 1971.

Baran, Paul A., and Sweezy, Paul M. *Monopoly Capital; An Essay on the American Economy and Social Order.* New York: Monthly Review Press, 1966.

Barbour, Floyd B. (ed.). *The Black Power Revolt: A Collection of Essays.* Boston: Porter Sargent, 1968.

Broderick, Francis L., and Meier, August (eds.). *Negro Protest Thought in the Twentieth Century.* Indianapolis, Ind.: Bobbs-Merrill Co., 1965.

Califano, Joseph A., Jr. *The Student Revolution: A Global Confrontation.* New York: W. W. Norton & Co., 1970.

Carmichael, Stokely, and Hamilton, Charles V. *Black Power; The Politics of Liberation in America.* New York: Vintage Books, 1967.

Chomsky, Noam. *American Power and the New Mandarins.* New York: Pantheon Books, 1969.

Cleaver, Eldridge. *Post-Prison Writings and Speeches.* Ed. Robert Scheer. New York: Random House, 1969.

———. *Soul on Ice.* New York: Dell Publishing Co., 1965.

Cohen, Mitchell, and Hale, Dennis (eds.). *The New Student Left: An Anthology.* Rev. and enl. ed. Boston: Beacon Press, 1967.

Cohn-Bendit, Daniel, et al. *The French Student Revolt; The Leaders Speak.* New York: Hill & Wang, 1968.

———, and Cohn-Bendit, Gabriel. *Obsolete Communism; The Left-Wing Alternative.* Trans. Arnold Pomerana. London: André Deutsch, 1968.

Cook, Terrence E., and Morgan, Patrick M. (eds.). *Participatory Democracy.* San Francisco: Canfield Press, 1971.

Cooper, David (ed.). *To Free a Generation; The Dialectics of Liberation.* New York: Collier Books, 1968.

Dahl, Robert A. *After the Revolution? Authority in a Good Society.* New Haven, Conn.: Yale University Press, 1970.

Draper, Hal. *Berkeley: The New Student Revolt.* New York: Grove Press, 1965.

Ehrenreich, Barbara, and Ehrenreich, John E. *Long March, Short Spring; The Student Uprising at Home and Abroad.* New York: Monthly Review Press, 1969.

Erlich, John, and Erlich, Susan (eds.). *Student Power, Participation and Revolution*. New York: Association Press, 1970.

Fanon, Frantz. *The Wretched of the Earth*. Trans. Constance Farrington. New York: Grove Press, 1963.

Gerberding, William P., and Smith, Duane E. (eds.). *The Radical Left: The Abuse of Discontent*. Boston: Houghton Mifflin, 1970.

Glazer, Nathan. *Remembering the Answers. Essays on the American Student Revolt*. New York: Basic Books, 1970.

Golembiewski, Robert T.; Bullock, Charles S., III; and Rodgers, Harrel R., Jr. *The New Politics: Polarization or Utopia?* New York: McGraw-Hill, 1970.

Goodman, Mitchell (comp.). *The Movement Toward a New America; The Beginning of a Long Revolution (A Collage) A What?* 1. *A Comprehension* 2. *A Compendium* 3. *A Handbook* 4. *A Guide* 5. *A History* 6. *A Revolution Kit* 7. *A Work-In-Progress*. Philadelphia: Pilgrim Press, 1970.

Gray, Francine duPlessix. *Divine Disobedience; Profiles in Catholic Radicalism*. New York: Vintage Books, 1970.

Greer, Edward (ed.). *Black Liberation Politics: A Reader*. Boston: Allyn and Bacon, 1971.

Hansberry, Lorraine. *The Movement; A Documentary of a Struggle for Equality*. New York: Simon and Schuster, 1964.

Hayden, Tom. *Rebellion and Repression*. New York: Meridian Books, 1969.

———. *Trial*. New York: Holt, Rinehart & Winston, 1970.

Hennessey, Caroline. *I, B.I.T.C.H.* New York: Lancer Books, 1970.

Hoffman, Abbie. *Revolution for the Hell of It* by Free (pseud.). New York: The Dial Press, 1968.

———. *Woodstock Nation; A Talk-Rock Album*. New York: Vintage Books, 1969.

Horowitz, David. *Student*. New York: Ballantine Books, 1962.

Jacobs, Paul, and Landau, Saul. *The New Radicals; A Report with Documents*. New York: Vintage Books, 1966.

Jaffe, Harold, and Tytell, John (eds.). *The American Experience; A Radical Reader*. New York: Harper & Row, 1970.

Jones, Beverley, and Brown, Judith. *Toward a Female Liberation Movement*. Boston: New England Free Press, n.d.

Keniston, Kenneth. *Young Radicals: Notes on Committed Youth*. New York: Harcourt, Brace & Jovanovich, 1968.

Kerouac, Jack. *The Dharma Bums*. New York: New American Library, 1958.

———. *On the Road*. New York: New American Library, 1957.

Kolko, Gabriel. *The Decline of American Radicalism in the Twentieth Century*. Boston: New England Free Press, n.d. Reprinted from the September/October, 1966 issue of *Studies on the Left*.

Kornbluth, Jesse (ed.). *Notes from the New Underground; An Anthology*. New York: The Viking Press, 1968.

Kunen, James Simon. *The Strawberry Statement: Notes of a College Revolutionary*. New York: Random House, 1968.

Lauter, Paul, and Howe, Florence. *The Conspiracy of the Young*. New York: World Publishing Co., 1970.

Lipset, Seymour Martin, and Wolin, Sheldon. (eds.). *The Berkeley Student Revolt; Facts and Interpretations*. Garden City, N.Y.: Doubleday & Co., 1965.

————, and Altbach, Philip G. (eds.). *Students in Revolt*. Boston: Houghton Mifflin, 1969. Winter 1968 issue of *Daedalus*.

Lipton, Lawrence. *The Holy Barbarians*. New York: Julian Meisner, 1959.

Long, Priscilla (ed.). *The New Left; A Collection of Essays*. Boston: Porter Sargent, 1969.

Lothstein, Arthur (ed.). *"All We Are Saying . . . ;" The Philosophy of The New Left*. New York: Capricorn Books, 1970.

McAfee, Kathy, and Wood, Myrna. *What is the Revolutionary Potential of Women's Liberation?* Boston: New England Free Press, n.d. Better known under title *Bread and Roses*. Appeared originally in the June, 1969 issue of *Leviathan*.

Mainardi, Pat. *The Politics of Housework*. Cambridge, Mass.: Betsy Warrior, n.d.

Marcuse, Herbert. *Eros and Civilization; A Philosophical Inquiry into Freud*. Boston: Beacon Press, 1955.

————. *An Essay on Liberation*. Boston: Beacon Press, 1969.

————. *Five Lectures; Psychoanalysis, Politics, and Utopia*. Trans. Jeremy J. Shapiro and Shierry M. Weber. Boston: Beacon Press, 1970.

————. *Negations: Essays in Critical Theory*. Trans. Jeremy J. Shapiro. Boston: Beacon Press, 1968.

————. *One Dimensional Man; Studies in the Ideology of Advanced Industrial Society*. Boston: Beacon Press, 1964.

Miller, Michael V., and Gilmore, Susan. (eds.). *Revolution at Berkeley*. New York: Dell, 1965.

Millett, Kate. *Sexual Politics*. Garden City, N.Y.: Doubleday & Co., 1970.

Morgan, Robin (ed.). *Sisterhood Is Powerful; An Anthology of Writings from the Women's Liberation Movement*. New York: Random House, 1970.

Nagel, Julian (ed.). *Student Power*. London: Merlin Press, 1969.

Newfield, Jack. *A Prophetic Minority*. New York: New American Library, 1966.

Oglesby, Carl, and Shaull, Richard. *Containment and Change*. New York: Macmillan, 1967.

——— (ed.). *The New Left Reader*. New York: Grove Press, 1969.

Powell, William. *The Anarchist Cookbook*. New York: Lyle Stuart, 1971.

Roszak, Theodore. *The Making of a Counter Culture; Reflections on the Technocratic Society and Its Youthful Opposition*. Garden City, N.Y.: Doubleday & Co., 1969.

Rubin, Jerry. *Do It! Scenarios of the Revolution*. New York: Simon and Schuster, 1970.

———. *We Are Everywhere*. New York: Harper & Row, 1971.

Silverman, Henry J. (ed.). *American Radical Thought; The Libertarian Tradition*. Lexington, Mass.: D. C. Heath & Co., 1970.

Silverman, Sondra (ed.). *The Black Revolt and Democratic Politics*. Lexington, Mass.: D. C. Heath & Co., 1970.

Storing, Herbert J. (ed.). *What Country Have I? Political Writings by Black Americans*. New York: St. Martin's Press, 1970.

Teodori, Massimo (ed.). *The New Left: A Documentary History*. Indianapolis, Ind.: Bobbs-Merrill Co., 1969.

Ware, Cellestine. *Woman Power; The Movement for Women's Liberation*. New York: Tower Publications, 1970.

Warshaw, Steven. *The Trouble in Berkeley*. Berkeley, Calif.: Diablo Press, 1965.

Wolfe, Tom. *The Electric Kool-Aid Acid Test*. New York: Bantam Books, 1968.

Young, Alfred F. (ed.). *Dissent; Explorations in the History of American Radicalism*. De Kalb, Ill.: Northern Illinois University Press, 1968.

Zinn, Howard. SNCC. *The New Abolitionists*. Boston: Beacon Press, 1965.

Periodicals have been particularly important in the development of New Left thought. Below is a short list of some of the more important ones. Some no longer exist, others may go out of existence or appear any time.

> *Guardian* (New Left from 1967 on.)
> *Monthly Review*
> *New Left Notes*
> *New Left Review*
> *Our Generation*
> *Radical America*
> *Studies on the Left*, 1959–67

8

ANARCHISM

The visibility of anarchism as an ideology has varied throughout this century. At one time anarchism was a household word in the United States, in the same way that communism is today. Because of the fear with which they were viewed at the beginning of the century, anarchists became the only group restricted from immigration into the United States on the basis of political beliefs. At other times, including the period from about 1930 into the 60s, little was heard of anarchism; it seemed to be a dead issue. On the other hand, today there is a growing interest in and popularity of anarchist thought. A number of collections of anarchist writings and studies of anarchism have appeared in the last few years.[1] Students rioting in Paris in June, 1968, carried the anarchist banner, not the Communist, and the black flag of anarchism is now frequently seen in demonstrations and protests. It can be said that anarchism is again a living ideology. It seems to be growing rapidly in England; it has adherents in Holland, France, and Latin America. It generally seems to be revitalized around the world.

---

[1] The studies include: George Woodcock, *Anarchism: A History of Libertarian Ideas and Movements* (Cleveland, Ohio: World Publishing Co., 1962); Daniel Guérin, *Anarchism From Theory to Practice*, trans., Mary Klopper (New York: Monthly Review Press, 1970); and James Joll, *The Anarchists* (London: Eyre & Spottiswoode, 1964). None of the collections in English warrants much attention, but the best is Leonard I. Krimerman and Lewis Perry, eds., *Patterns of Anarchy; A Collection of Writings on the Anarchist Tradition* (Garden City, N.Y.: Doubleday Anchor Books, 1966). See the selected readings at the end of the chapter for further material.

Principles of anarchism

The ideology that we call anarchism has a wide variety of forms and ideas. The purpose of the chapter will be to explore the principles of anarchism in an effort to understand the appeal of anarchism and the reaction against it. Most studies of anarchism have focused on a select group of men, usually Prince Peter Kropotkin, Pierre-Joseph Proudhon, Mikhail Bakunin, Count Leo Tolstoi, Max Stirner, William Godwin, Georges Sorel, and William Morris, with sometimes a bow in the direction of a few lesser figures such as Errico Malatesta, Elisée Reclus, Benjamin Tucker, and Josiah Warren. This approach may produce a valid presentation and analysis of the clusters of ideas that make up anarchism, but it is equally likely to result in a total misunderstanding of the important similarities and the equally important differences among anarchists. The best approach, therefore, seems to be to select those parts of the anarchist tradition that are most important today while striving to maintain a balanced presentation. We shall deal with three schools of anarchism: communist anarchism, anarcho-syndicalism, and individualist anarchism. The first two constitute the major components of contemporary anarchist thought; the third, a permanent minority position, will be discussed in order to illustrate the full range of anarchist ideas.

It is possible to make a few generalizations about anarchism as a whole, although individualist anarchism does not always fit. Kropotkin once defined anarchism as:

. . . the name given to a principle or theory of life and conduct under which society is conceived without government—harmony in such a society being obtained, not by submission to law or by obedience to any authority, but by free agreements concluded between the various groups, territorial and professional, freely constituted for the sake of production and consumption, as also for the satisfaction of the infinite variety of needs and aspirations of a civilized being.[2]

Voluntary associations are basic to anarchism, but this is often forgotten or unknown.[3] Anarchism is, then, a political philosophy that argues that no group in society should have coercive authority over the society as a

---

[2] Peter Kropotkin, "Anarchism," *Encyclopaedia Britannica,* 11th ed. (Cambridge, Eng.: Cambridge University Press, 1910), vol. I, p. 914.

[3] Although the individualist anarchist does not emphasize voluntary associations, they do not reject them altogether.

whole and, on the positive side, that society should be composed of a wide variety of groups designed to coordinate the functions that are essential to the operation of any society. Anarchists differ somewhat on the inter-relationships among these groups and on the importance of particular groups in the social system, but they would agree, with some reservations, with this definition. Most anarchists would also agree that it is the working class or proletariat that provides the basis for anarchist support and the future society. A few anarchists take exception to this approach—correctly, it may be argued.[4] Since this is not the place to settle debates within anarchism, we will move on.

The word *anarchy* comes from the Greek *anarchos* meaning without a head or chief, and many anarchists trace the development of the doctrine from Greek philosophy, particularly Cynicism.[5] In addition to tracing anarchist thought back to the Greeks, it is often argued that examples of the basic notions and concepts of anarchism can be found throughout the history of political philosophy in both Western and non-Western cultures. But, be that as it may, the real history of anarchism begins in fairly recent times. The first individual to call himself an anarchist was Pierre-Joseph Proudhon (1809–65). Prior to Proudhon there were a number of other thinkers that clearly fell within the anarchist mold.

Anarchism has always been attacked on the basis of its advocacy of violence and chaos. There have been certain anarchists, clearly a minority, who we label direct action anarchists, who have believed that the only way to achieve the ideal anarchist society is through the physical destruction of contemporary society. They have advocated individual acts of terrorism and assassination. They are the ones who led to a stereotype of the anarchist as a man in a heavy black beard carrying a bomb. There have been incidents of violence connected with anarchists in the past, both in the United States and abroad. On the other hand, the major portion of anarchist thought has always been in the direction of what is called philosophical anarchism. Philosophical anarchism is basically a nonviolent doctrine, although some anarchists of this mold believe that a violent

---

[4] On this problem see John Pilgrim, "Salvation by the Working Class: Is It an Outmoded Myth?," *Anarchy* 68 (October, 1966), pp. 289–300, and Arthur Uloth, "Anarchism, the Workers, and Social Revolution," *Anarchy* 74 (April, 1967), pp. 114–16.

[5] See, for example, D. Ferraro, "Anarchism in Greek Philosophy," *Anarchy* 45, Vol. IV (November, 1964), pp. 321–35. Reprinted from *The Pluralist*.

revolution is inevitable even though it is not desirable. Hence, the history of anarchism is spotted with incidents of destruction and violence, but it should be kept in mind that the major figures in the history of anarchism tended to advocate nonviolence rather than violence.

At the same time, a doctrine that advocates a social system primarily characterized by the disappearance of certain of the major institutions of contemporary society might well be expected to advocate violent change. We find, for example, such writers as William Morris saying that anarchism can only come about after a period of violent revolution. Interestingly enough, Morris' main work is subtitled "An Epoch of Rest," which illustrates a key problem for the anarchist. Anarchist society is most clearly conceived as a peaceful society—one in which conflicts among individuals or groups within the society are worked out among those individuals or groups without resort to any physical force. Still, many anarchists argue that such a society can only be brought about through violence.

The key here is found in the anarchists' characterization of contemporary society and particularly the political system which they hope will disappear. They argue, and some scholars of politics would agree with them, that the major characterization of a political system or a government is its ability to legitimately use violence to enforce its commands. Since anarchism advocates doing away with government, it would be expected, and certainly would be expected by an anarchist, that the government would use this ability to use physical force against any attempt, no matter how motivated, to abolish itself. Therefore, the anarchist can argue with some validity that even though he would desire a process of peaceful change, a violent revolution would be forced upon him by the very nature of contemporary society.

Thus, one of the key debates in the history of anarchist thought has been over violence versus nonviolence. This debate is by no means ended, and we shall see it again as we look at certain of the contemporary themes in anarchist thought. In addition to the debate over this tactic, a number of other controversies within the history of anarchist thought help to illuminate it. We have already mentioned the question of the role of the proletariat in the making of the anarchist revolution, and it should be noted that this question has been outside of the realm of debate in anarchist thought until very recently. Historically, it can be said that anarchists have almost universally viewed the proletariat as a revolutionary or potentially revolutionary class. They have seen in the proletariat the basis of the possible future society and the means of achieving it through revolution.

The attitude of anarchists toward the proletariat can be found expressed in a short utopian novel called *The Sorcery Shop*.[6] This novel presents a world without government and a world in which labor and the laborer are highly respected. The individual in the utopia of this novel is one who develops fully his potential as an individual and as a human being because he is allowed to develop in his own way and along the lines of his own interests. It is contended that such freedom will produce a well-rounded individual. It is believed that anyone living in a society in which physical labor is not denigrated will participate in some such labor for a wide variety of reasons; he might take on ditchdigging, for example, rather like a modern man takes on jogging. In addition, it is believed that everyone in the society will cooperate in order to undertake tasks that are in the common interest. For example, if a community desires a town hall or meeting place or a theater the individuals in the community will get together and pool their talents and build it themselves. The point is that, where physical labor and the laborer are respected, all people will develop some skills along these lines and will readily contribute to the good of the entire community. No one will have to work long, dreary hours at a job that he does not like. Everyone will be able to work at what he likes when he likes, and a spirit of cooperation will enrich all communal activities and will form the true community in which individuals will be able to freely work together for the good of the whole.

The reason for this attitude toward the proletariat on the part of the anarchist may be found in the way that anarchism developed alongside the industrial revolution. Anarchists and others, such as Marx, saw in the conditions of the 19th century a dehumanizing force that attacked all men but particularly the proletariat. Both Marx and the anarchists were concerned with achieving human emancipation. Both believed that it could not be done through a political state. As anarchism developed and as industrialism became stronger and stronger as a force in society, the anarchists came to believe that all men, once freed from the conditions imposed by government, would be capable of cooperation and community. This is a key difference between Marx and the anarchists.

---

[6] Robert Blatchford, *The Sorcery Shop; An Impossible Romance* (London: Clarion Press, 1909).

From the Marxian point of view, the anarchists were attacking a part of the superstructure, the state, which was merely a product of the economic environment. Thus, again from the Marxian point of view, the anarchists were doomed to failure from the very beginning. They failed to recognize what was the true cause of the condition. They were merely treating an effect. The anarchists argued, on the other hand, that the state was not merely an effect of the economic system. They believed that the key element in society was not economic relations but coercion. And the state or the government was the symbol of coercion and the institution of society that had ultimate power over the individuals within it. Anarchists believed that if they could merely be rid of the state, man's better nature, which had been suppressed through coercion, would be able to come out again. They believed that ridding society of coercion would be the humanizing force.

The anarchists also recognized, in most cases, that there was something basically wrong with the economic system. They generally accepted the socialist economic system as the solution to the economic problem. They argued, of course, that this socialist system must be run by the workers themselves. At the same time, many anarchists viewed the industrial system as inherently pernicious, and they argued that the only solution would be to do away with this system and return to an agrarian economy. The debate over the economic system is today a crucial one and splits anarchism into two wings. Today anarchists are not universally agreed on the desirability of socialism as an economic system. Some, a small minority, believe that only capitalism can appropriately be combined with anarchism. There are a few left today who wish to return to an agrarian economy, although there are some signs that that few may be growing. The problem of the economic system that best fits anarchism will be discussed somewhat further after we look at some of the modern systems of anarchist thought.

Of course, the key element in all anarchism is the rejection of any imposed method of life. All anarchists contend that the life style of the individual must be chosen by the individual and not forced upon him. Historically, most anarchists have believed that individuals within a society that was free of coercion would be able to live a highly moral life. Today most anarchists would argue that an individual's morality is solely an individual question. At the same time, most anarchists argue that the greatest freedom must be allowed for choice among widely divergent life styles and that no pressure of any sort must be put on an individual's choice.

Communist anarchism

Communist anarchism is most often identified with the theories of Kropotkin, and he certainly was the best-known exponent of the position, but two other men present the ideas as clearly and concisely. Alexander Berkman says, "Anarchism teaches that we can live in a society where there is no compulsion of any kind. A life without compulsion naturally means liberty; it means freedom from being forced or coerced, a chance to lead the life that suits you best."[7] In order to do this, Berkman argues, it is necessary to get rid of government and capitalism and replace them with liberty and equality of use; according to him this would produce communist anarchism.[8] The key to Berkman's approach to anarchism is his emphasis on the need to develop a society without compulsion or coercion. He believes that contemporary society, with its emphasis on economic inequality, produces a system in which it is impossible for an individual to act freely. He contends that capitalism and any form of government strike at man's ability to be free. The capitalist system does it by insuring economic inequality, and government does it through the plethora of laws that limit men's activities. The anarchist would argue that these laws, many of which are designed to maintain individual liberty, in fact limit this liberty even when attempting to maintain it. They do this by so controlling men that they are incapable of acting decently to one another. Government and law and capitalism thus are, for Berkman, the roots of all evil.

Herbert Read bases his discussion of anarchism on the principle of equity and contends that this principle is best illustrated by "analogies derived from the simplicity and harmony of universal physical laws. . . ."[9] These analogies of physical laws are derived in part from Kropotkin's pioneering work *Mutual Aid* in which he argued on the basis of empirical evidence that cooperation within the species rather than conflict is common

---

[7] Alexander Berkman, *ABC of Anarchism*, 3rd ed. (London: Freedom Press, 1964), p. 10.

[8] Ibid., p. 12.

[9] Herbert Read, *The Philosophy of Anarchism* (London: Freedom Press, 1940), p. 17.

to all species. Therefore, he contended that man could follow this natural law and, by cooperating with his fellow human beings, could do away with coercive institutions such as government. This scientific anarchism, as it is called, is the basis for many of the more contemporary approaches to anarchism. Although Kropotkin's approach through the idea of the co-operation within species is generally accepted by anarchists today, it is not a major focus of concern. Contemporary anarchists are not primarily concerned with proving the scientific basis of anarchism, but, assuming that it exists, they attempt to show specific ways in contemporary society where cooperation is possible. Ultimately, they, like Read, believe that the ultimate level of cooperation will only be possible when man is capable of doing away with coercive institutions.

But communist anarchism and anarchism in general is something more than a set of glittering generalities in favor of liberty and equality and against government and capitalism. As noted in Kropotkin's definition, the positive content of anarchism, particularly communist anarchism and syn-dicalism, focuses on voluntary associations. These associations are obvi-ously of many kinds, and it is difficult to easily generalize about them. One way of viewing the anarchist system is to look at William Morris' utopian novel, *News From Nowhere* (1891). Morris was a communist anarchist; his philosophy consists of:

1. No government and no coercion
2. An agricultural and craft economy
3. All goods freely available to all
4. Highly developed sense of individual cooperation

In his novel, Morris presents a beautiful picture of a land in which co-operation does exist. In this land, people meet together and decide that something needs to be done that requires a certain amount of physical labor and then go and do it without any bureaucracy regulating their work. During harvest time, people go out into the fields for the enjoyment of working.

This land of Morris' is a utopia and it is consciously described as such. At the same time, it is the land that Morris and many other anarchists believe to be possible if man can get rid of government and capitalism. Modern anarchists are seldom concerned with a purely agricultural and craft economy but with an industrial-based economy. There is an exception to this rejection of the agricultural economy among those anarchists who believe in the Green Revolution. These anarchists favor a return to the land and an intensive cultivation of the land in order to provide sufficient food for themselves. They believe that land can be cultivated carefully enough so that it is possible to support the population that the world holds today. They believe that the life of the cities and the industries is corrupting, that man cannot cooperate in such conditions, and that only if man returns to the land will anarchism ever be possible. Most contemporary anarchists accept the syndicalist solution to this problem, which will be discussed later.

The key to Morris' system is point four. Without the ability to cooperate, his system, and anarchism, must appear extremely naïve. We know that men can cooperate. We do not know whether or not an entire society can be based solely on cooperation, but it is the basic postulate of anarchism that this is possible. There is a partial exception to this in individualist anarchism, which we will discuss later, but most anarchists consider individualist anarchism impossible and undesirable. The communist anarchist is arguing for a voluntary association of individuals that will form a society. Thus, for the communist anarchist all society is in the form of voluntary associations. For the communist anarchist there is no essential group such as the proletariat that necessarily forms the basis of the society. For the communist anarchist all individuals associate equally together, and they do not have the class bias that one finds often in anarcho-syndicalism.

The communist anarchist believes that an individual should be free to choose for himself the forms of association that he has with other individuals. Thus, they do not insist upon any particular form of marriage relationship or even any marriage relationship at all. There is no proscription of any sexual activity. There is no set system of education, although communist anarchism has often been in the forefront of experimentation in education. Thus, also, there is no proscription or support of religion. There is within anarchist circles considerable debate over the question of religious affiliation for an anarchist. Many argue that this is incompatible with anarchism, whereas others argue that it depends on the type of organization or church.

Still others, including the Catholic anarchists, such as Dorothy Day and Ammon Hennacy, who left the church shortly before he died, argue that the faith in the doctrines of the church do not affect them as anarchists

—that the church only speaks on matters of faith and morals; that it does not deal with the rest of their lives. Outside of these areas the Catholic anarchist considers himself to be completely free from the church. The Catholic anarchist is merely a special case of contemporary communist anarchism. The individuals such as Dorothy Day and, for a time, Ammon Hennacy, who accept a highly authoritarian religion and at the same time consider themselves anarchists, are merely taking one part of their life, that part that deals with questions of religious faith, and accepting the dictates of the church. This faith, as long as it is restricted to religious questions and perhaps also moral questions, does not necessarily affect the social and political positions of the anarchist. It obviously could affect these positions in relationship to questions of morals, but this would depend on the individual's own temperament. Thus, the emphasis of communist anarchism is on voluntary association of individuals in a variety of forms, one of which is the commune or the society which makes cooperatively and by consensus whatever political decisions must be made.

Anarcho-syndicalism

One of the approaches to cooperation is syndicalism or anarcho-syndicalism. The basic principles are as follows:

1. Each industry is organized into a federation of independent communes.
2. Each industry is controlled by the workers in that industry.[10]
3. Policy questions and questions of intercommune relations handled by a coordinating council which, having no powers delegated to it, acts solely as an arbiter.[11]

This summary of anarcho-syndicalism should make two points very clear. First, anarchism is not simply a rejection of government and an acceptance of complete individualism. Second, anarchism has within it a theory or theories of organization.

The key to an understanding of anarcho-syndicalism is found in its industrial base. The central element of anarcho-syndicalism is workers' control. The society is organized on the basis of the control of each industry by the workers in that industry. The word *industry* is normally defined

---

[10] On workers control see *Anarchy* 2 (April, 1961).
[11] Read, *The Philosophy of Anarchism*, pp. 26–27.

quite broadly by the anarcho-syndicalists to include such activities as the building industry, which then would be controlled by all of the different workers who participate in building any structure. Thus, these individuals, according to anarcho-syndicalism, come together to decide on the particular problems of that industry. Then representatives of each industry get together and administer the economic life of the entire country. The key word here is *administer*.

This is the same thing as Engels' statement that in the final stage of communism, the government of men will change to the administration of things. Men in anarcho-syndicalism will no longer be governed. Men will be free from government, but they will participate in administering the economic life of the country. The contention is that there is essentially no such thing as a political decision. The administration of things should be, according to anarcho-syndicalism, a fairly simple and mechanical operation which will not give rise to many conflicts that will have to be ironed out. When conflicts do arise because of the problems of allocating scarce goods, the workers, who are the people that most industries serve, will be the ones in the best positions to know what is most important, what can be produced most inexpensively, how to improve production; thus, these people are the ones who should be making these decisions rather than the managers who are not in contact with the actual work. The anarcho-syndicalist also argues that putting the worker in control of his own job will enable him to produce more, thus lessening the problem of the allocation of scarce goods. The anarcho-syndicalist thus argues that workers' control acts as a great incentive to work.

Some anarcho-syndicalists have argued that the basis for the new society is to be found in the organization of the present trade unions. However, modern anarcho-syndicalists view the trade unions as essentially conservative groups, particularly in the leadership, that are directly opposed to any possibility of workers' control. Thus, modern anarcho-syndicalists are often in opposition to the union movement and see the unions cooperating with industry and government rather than opposing them for the benefit of the worker. Thus, although the idea of syndicalism originated as part of the trade-union movement in France, it has in its form of anarcho-syndicalism moved away from the movement and tends today to be in opposition to it. It still does, though, base itself on the proletariat.

The differences between communist anarchism and anarcho-syndicalism are not great. Anarcho-syndicalism is more directly concerned with the organization of industrial society than is communist anarchism, but both of them come to fundamentally the same conclusions. Both of them accept the notion that the workers in a given area should control the operation of that area, whether it be a commune as in communist anarchism or an industry as in anarcho-syndicalism, for the benefit of the society as a whole. It is assumed in both cases that the entire population will be workers, at least to the extent that they will be participating to some degree in the economic life of the society. Both of them believe that by removing coercion a viable society can operate. The difference is primarily found in the emphasis of anarcho-syndicalism on the operation of the industrial system.

Anarcho-syndicalism and communist anarchism developed a secondary level of organization that is also important for understanding the course of anarchist thought. Both types of anarchism stress the need for some way of developing cooperation among communes or industries as well as within the individual commune or industry. Although the focus of most studies of anarchist thought has been on the individual and his freedom gained through the destruction of coercion, the anarchists have always argued that it is not possible to stop there. Except for the individualist anarchists, who will be discussed shortly, the primary focus of anarchism does not rest on the isolated individual. The focus of anarchism is on an individual within a noncoercive society. The emphasis is on producing the type of society that will allow the individual to be free. Most anarchists recognize that the small commune or industry is not sufficient for man in contemporary society. They have recognized that some cooperation is necessary among communes and industries in order to produce sufficient goods in sufficient diversity for each individual.

This is most clearly recognized in anarcho-syndicalism because its basic form of organization, the industry, is specialized. Therefore, in order to give each individual the goods that are necessary for his life, there must be a high degree of cooperation among the industries to provide a sufficient distribution system for the goods produced by the individual industries. Again, it is argued that the only way to handle this is through cooperation on the part of the workers within the various industries. To some extent it could be argued that what is looked for here is simply a form of enlightened self-interest, because each individual worker in a particular industry does himself need the products of a wide variety of industries. Therefore, in order to achieve this the individual workers will cooperate with workers from a wide variety of industries, because they all need the products of each and every industry. The anarcho-syndicalists believe that this co-operation can be developed readily once coercion disappears. This belief is held, it seems, primarily because it is believed that such cooperation will be to the advantage of all the individuals within the society.

Individualist anarchism

Arguing that anarchism is not an acceptance of complete individualism, we are ignoring an interesting minority group among anarchists, individualist anarchists. The feeling of individualist anarchism can be seen in this poem by Pat Parker, the wife of one of the very few living theorists of this school of thought.

> ask the help of great god
> there is no great god
> there is no god
> there is no damned help
>
> there is myself
> there is my everlasting desperate self
> there is almighty me
> omnipresent
> all-creative
> master of everything
> lord of the skies
> me.[12]

The philosophy of individualist anarchism is best seen in the following statement by S. E. Parker:

Individualism

"Individualism" is one of those words like "anarchism" and "egoism" that have been abused out of both ignorance and intent. For many radicals it is a synonym for the "free-for-all" of the "capitalist jungle," and some defenders of capitalism have tried to use it to justify economic exploitation and monopoly. A little intelligent thinking about the nature of capitalist society, however, is enough to upset this idea. What is *individual* about the armies of city gentlemen marching into and out of their offices at the same time five days a week and vegetating in the cage of their suburban conventions in between? And

---

[12] Pat Parker, *Some Poems* (London: S. E. Parker, 1966).

how *individual* are the herds of industrial workers standing before the machine-god and repeating the same servile rituals throughout their lives?

Individualist-anarchism

Individualism is something quite different from the caricature common to both "Left" and "Right."

> "It is the recognition by the individual that he is above all institutions and formulas; that these exist only so far as he chooses to make them his own by accepting them." (*John Beverly Robinson*)

Because they regard no institution or formula as having authority over them, individualists are logically anarchists. And because they deny the validity of any authority external to the individual, anarchists are logically individualists. From this awareness is born an anarchism freed from the last vestiges of that altruistic idealism which casts out service to God and the State only to replace it with service to the Cause and Humanity. Individualist-anarchism drives authority out of its last hiding place in "moral obligation" or "duty." Individualist-anarchists are philosophically egoists.[13]

The individualist anarchist does not completely reject cooperation between men. He argues that cooperation is essential for the fulfillment of some needs. But he contends that only the individualist, the true individualist as he defines him, is capable of genuinely forming a voluntary association with others. In addition, he never sees this association as an end in itself but merely as a useful form for a temporary purpose. It must be the servant of the members, not dominate the members.

The individualist anarchist argues against the collective ownership of goods, but he is not convinced that the capitalist system is any better. Here one finds a major split in the ranks of individualist anarchists—on the one hand, there are those such as S. E. Parker who reject both capitalism and socialism and argue that they are not yet convinced that either system is valid within an individualist anarchist environment. In a review of this section of the first edition of this book, he says, ". . . I do tend to believe these days that there is far more hope of a consistent individualism emerging from the 'free market' approach than from the 'free-communist' approach, most of whose advocates are heavily sold on collectivism."[14] On the other hand, there are those who are labeled right-wing individualists

---

[13] S. E. Parker, *Individualist Anarchism: An Outline* (London: S. E. Parker, 1965), p. 1.

[14] S. E. Parker, "Review of *Contemporary Political Ideologies; A Comparative Analysis,*" *Minus One; An Individualist Anarchist Review*, 25 (December, 1969), p. 11.

or libertarians, who contend that the only form of economic life compatible with individualism is capitalism. Usually their approach is connected with a view of life rather like that of the Social Darwinist. They see life as a struggle for survival between men and hold that a socialist economic system keeps alive those who do not deserve to survive.

Individualist anarchism is changing. The right-wing individualists and the left-wing individualists are finding more and more that they have much in common. Still, there are significant differences that remain. Right-wing individualists in the United States still have the vestiges of an only recently discarded patriotism. Left-wing individualists have never been touched significantly by patriotism. Shortly, I expect that the designations left and right as applied to individualists will become meaningless.

All of anarchism, whether communist, anarcho-syndicalist, or individualist, is concerned with the freedom of the individual. Anarchism is a system of thought that rejects control by any group but particularly by the organized group we call the state or the government. Anarchists argue that men are capable of freedom and that they are capable of cooperating together in voluntary association. They believe that men are willing and able to help each other. They believe that man's best instincts are destroyed by the present organization of society. They feel, as did Marx, that true love between individuals is impossible, or at least very difficult, under contemporary conditions. They feel that a morality system that rejects physical relationships without the sanction of church and state destroys the possibility of developing what Marx called the love-sex relationship. The anarchist does not insist upon or reject the simple monogamous marriage relationship. Individuals, they contend, must decide on what sort of relationship they want to live in. It is their life, and they must be free to make these sorts of decisions.

The anarchist also contends that there is a real responsibility on the part of parents in such a relationship to insure freedom for their children. They feel that the contemporary educational system is destructive of freedom and creativity and any possibility of learning. They feel that there must be some type of educational system that is directed to the individual child, whatever his needs may be. This cannot be found, they believe, in the highly organized, overly complex educational system that we have today. It can be found in the small group that is concerned with educating for freedom; that does not convince itself that education is the ingestion of a myriad of facts that may not be relevant to the particular child's interest.

They believe that a child given the freedom to choose and select and given the encouragement to follow his own bent will gradually find what interests him and, getting interested, will apply the tremendous energies that children can develop to a study, an understanding, and a learning of those things that interest him.

Much of what we are taught in our schools, the anarchist believes, is totally irrelevant to our lives; we waste many years in attempting to learn things that we will really never be interested in. A child should be encouraged to look at the world and interpret it on his own rather than being given answers. This approach to education puts a tremendous burden on the parent and the teacher. The teacher must develop a close relationship with the child in order to be able to understand the child's changing interests and to suggest to the child ways in which he might best fulfill his current interest. This must be done without directing the child too much. The parent also must be capable of giving the child freedom. The parent must not control the child too much. Anarchist theories of child rearing and education have been some of the most innovative, instructive, and successful of any of the anarchist approaches to contemporary life.

Anarchism will probably always remain a minor ideology. It is unlikely that anarchism will ever succeed in this world, but anarchism is essentially a humanistic belief in man. Anarchism is the ideology that has the most faith in man. It believes as no other ideology does that man is capable of freedom and cooperation.

Suggested readings

Aldred, Guy. *Bakunin*. Glasgow: The Strickland Press, 1940.

——— (ed.). *Bakunin's Writings*. Indore, India: Modern Publishers, n.d.

Armand, E. *Anarchism and Individualism: Three Essays*. Trans. D. T. W. London: S. E. Parker, n.d.

———. *What Individualist-Anarchists Want*. Trans. Mark William Kramrisch. Adapted by S. E. Parker. London: S. E. Parker, n.d.

Avrich, Paul. *The Russian Anarchists*. Princeton, N.J.: Princeton University Press, 1967.

Bakunin, Mikhail. *God and the State*. New York: Dover Publications, 1970.

———. *Marxism, Freedom and the State*. Ed. and trans. K. J. Kenafick. London: Freedom Press, 1950.

———. *The Political Philosophy of Bakunin: Scientific Anarchism*. Comp. and ed. G. P. Maximoff. New York: The Free Press, 1953.

Barrett, George (pseud. for George Powell Ballard). *The First Person*. London: Freedom Press, 1963.

Berkman, Alexander. *ABC of Anarchism*. 3d ed. London: Freedom Press, 1964.

Berneri, C. *Peter Kropotkin; His Federalist Ideas*. London: Freedom Press, 1942.

Brailsford, H. N. *Shelley, Godwin, and Their Circle*. New York: Henry Holt & Co., n.d.

Carr, E. G. *Michael Bakunin*. New York: Vintage Books, 1937.

Christie, Stuart, and Meltzer, Albert. *The Floodgates of Anarchy*. London: Kahn & Averill, 1970.

De Cleyre, Voltairine. *Selected Works of Voltairine de Cleyre*. Ed. Alexander Berkman. New York: Mother Earth Publishing Co., 1914.

De Lubac, Henri, S. J. *The Un-Marxian Socialist: A Study of Proudhon*. Trans. R. E. Scantlebury. New York: Sheed & Ward, 1948.

Devaldes, Manuel. *Reflexions sur l'individualisme*. Paris: Editions Pensee et Action, 1958.

Eltzbacher, Paul. *Anarchism; Exponents of the Anarchist Philosophy*. Trans. Steven T. Byington. Ed. James J. Martin. London: Freedom Press, 1960.

Godwin, William. *Enquiry Concerning Political Justice and Its Influence on Morals and Happiness*. Ed. F. E. L. Priestley. 3 vols. Toronto: University of Toronto Press, 1946.

Goldman, Emma. *Anarchism and Other Essays*. New York: Dover Publications, 1970.

———. *Living My Life*. 2 vols. New York: Dover Publications, 1970.

Goodman, Paul (ed.). *Seeds of Liberation*. New York: George Braziller, 1964.

Guérin, Daniel. *Anarchism From Theory to Practice*. Trans. Mary Klopper New York: Monthly Review Press, 1970.

Hennacy, Ammon. *The Book of Ammon*. The Author, 1965.

Hoffman, Robert (ed.). *Anarchism*. New York: Atherton Press, 1970.

Horowitz, Irving L. (ed.). *The Anarchists*. New York: Dell Publishing Co., 1964.

Joll, James. *The Anarchists*. London: Eyre & Spottiswoode, 1964.

Kornbluth, Joyce L. (ed.). *Rebel Voices; An I.W.W. Anthology*. Ann Arbor: The University of Michigan Press, 1968.

Krimerman, Leonard I., and Perry, Lewis (eds.). *Patterns of Anarchy: A Collection of Writings on the Anarchist Tradition*. Garden City, N.Y.: Doubleday & Co., 1966.

Kropotkin, Peter. *The Conquest of Bread*. New York: G. P. Putnam's Sons, 1907.

————. *Ethics: Origin and Development*. Trans. Louis S. Friedland and Joseph R. Piroshnikoff. New York: Tudor Publishing Co., 1924.

————. *Fields, Factories and Workshops*. New York: Benjamin Blom, 1968.

————. *The Great French Revolution 1789–1793*. 2 vols. Trans. N. F. Dryhurst. New York: Vanguard Press, 1909.

————. *Kropotkin's Revolutionary Pamphlets*. Ed. Roger N. Baldwin. New York: Dover Publications, 1970.

————. *Memoirs of a Revolutionist*. Ed. James Allen Rogers. Garden City, N.Y.: Doubleday & Co., 1962.

————. *Mutual Aid; A Factor of Evolution*. Boston: Extending Horizons Books, 1955.

————. *Organised Vengeance Called "Justice."* 2nd ed. London: Freedom Press, 1948.

————. *Selected Writings on Anarchism and Revolution*. Ed. Martin A. Miller. Cambridge, Mass.: The M.I.T. Press, 1970.

————. *The Wage System*. London: Freedom Press, n.d.

————. *War!* 7th ed. London: William Reeves, n.d.

Malatesta, Errico. *Anarchy*. 8th ed. London: Freedom Press, 1949.

————. "A Talk Between Two Workers," n.p., 1933, pamphlet.

————. *Vote What For?* 3rd ed. New York: Libertarian League, 1959.

Martin, James J. *Men Against the State: The Expositors of Individualist Anarchism in America, 1827–1908*. Colorado Springs, Colo.: Ralph Myles, 1970.

Maryson, Dr. J. A. *The Principles of Anarchism*. Trans. A. Grossner. New York: Jewish Anarchist Federation of America, 1935.

Morris, William. *News from Nowhere or An Epoch of Rest; Being Some Chapters from a Utopian Romance*. Chicago: Charles H. Kerr, n.d.

Nettlau, M. *Bibliographie de l'anarchie*. New York: Burt Franklin, 1968.

Ni Dieu ni maitre. Anthologie historique du mouvement anarchiste. Paris: Editions de Delphes, 1965.

Parker, Pat. *Some Poems*. London: S. E. Parker, 1966.

Parker, S. E. *Individualist Anarchism: An Outline*. London: S. E. Parker, 1965.

Proudhon, Pierre-Joseph. *General Idea of the Revolution in the Nineteenth Century*. Trans. John Beverley Robinson. London: Freedom Press, 1923.

————. *Oeuvres choisies*. Paris: Gallimard, 1967.

————. *Selected Writings of P.-J. Proudhon*. Ed. Stewart Edwards. Trans. Elizabeth Fraser. Garden City, N.Y.: Doubleday Anchor Books, 1969.

————. *What is Property: An Inquiry into the Principle of Right and of*

Government. 2 vols. in one. Trans. Benjamin R. Tucker. London: William Reeves, n.d.

Read, Herbert. *Anarchy and Order; Essays in Politics.* London: Faber & Faber, 1954.

————. *The Education of Free Men.* London: Freedom Press, 1944.

————. *The Philosophy of Anarchism.* London: Freedom Press, 1940.

————. *Poetry and Anarchism.* 2nd ed. London: Freedom Press, 1947.

Richards, Vernon (comp. and ed.). *Errico Malatesta; His Life and Ideas.* London: Freedom Press, 1965.

Rocker, Rudolf. *Nationalism and Culture.* Trans. Ray E. Chase. Los Angeles: Rocker Publications Committee, 1937.

Russell, Bertrand. *Roads to Freedom: Socialism, Anarchism and Syndicalism.* 3rd ed. London: George Allen & Unwin, 1920.

Schweitzer, Jean-Pierre. *O Idios; Three Essays on Individualist Anarchism.* London: S. E. Parker, 1966.

Stirner, Max. *The Ego and His Own: The Case of the Individual Against Authority.* Trans. Steven T. Byington. Ed. James M. Martin. New York: Libertarian Book Club, 1963.

————. *The False Principle of Our Education or Humanism and Realism.* Trans. Robert H. Beebe. Ed. James J. Martin. Colorado Springs, Colo.: Ralph Myles, 1967.

Tolstoy, Leo. *The Law of Love and the Law of Violence.* Trans. Mary Koutouzow Tolstoy. London: Anthony Blond, 1970.

Tucker, Benjamin R. *Individual Liberty; Selections from the Writings of Benjamin R. Tucker.* Ed. C.L.S. New York: Vanguard Press, 1926.

Woodcock, George. *Anarchism; A History of Libertarian Ideas and Movements.* Cleveland, Ohio: World Publishing Co., 1962.

————. *Anarchy or Chaos.* London: Freedom Press, 1944.

————. *Pierre-Joseph Proudhon: A Biography.* London: Routledge & Kegan Paul, 1956.

————. *What Is Anarchism?* New York: Libertarian League, n.d.

————. *William Godwin: A Biographical Study.* London: Porcupine Press, 1946.

————. *The Writer and Politics.* London: Porcupine Press, 1948.

————, and Avakumovic, Ivan. *The Anarchist Prince; A Biographical Study of Peter Kropotkin.* London: T. V. Broadman, 1950.

Woolf, Robert Paul. *In Defense of Anarchism.* New York: Harper & Row, 1970.

Zaccaria, C. *William Godwin, le constructeur. Federations de personnes.* Paris: Editions Pensee & Action, 1953.

9
CONCLUSION

We have dealt with seven sets of ideologies in this book. It is important to note that each is a set of ideologies and not in any case a monolithic position free of disagreements. We have indicated major disagreements and differences of opinion in connection with all of them. I have attempted in this final chapter to compare these ideologies with regard to two sets of categories—one directed at questions of political philosophy, the other directed at the various parts of the social system. Therefore a comparison has to be very general, while attempting to avoid being too broad and therefore meaningless.

Below is a series of questions designed to provide a fairly complete analysis of the assumptions of a political ideology. By using a set of questions like this, it is possible to compare the ideologies.

   I. Human Nature
       A. What are the basic characteristics of man as man?
       B. What effect does the nature of man have upon the political system?
  II. The Origin of Society and Government or the State
       A. What is the origin of society? Why does it develop?
       B. What is the origin of government or the state? Why does it develop?
 III. Political Obligation (Duty, Responsibility, Law)
       A. Why does man obey the government?
       B. Why should man obey the government, or should he at all?
       C. Is disobedience ever justifiable?

D. Is revolution ever justifiable?

IV. Liberty (Rights—Substantive and Procedural)

A. Is man free in any way vis-à-vis the government?

B. Should man be free vis-à-vis the government?

C. Assuming that some type or types of freedom are both possible and desirable, what should these be? Should they be limited or unlimited? Who places limits?

V. Equality

A. Are men in any way "naturally" equal?

B. Should men be in any way equal?

C. Assuming that some type or types of equality are both possible and desirable, what should these be? Should they be absolute or relative? If relative, what criteria should be used to establish them? Who establishes the criteria? Who enforces the criteria?

VI. Community (Fraternity)

A. Is there any existing form of human society that logically precedes or is in any way above the individuals that compose it?

B. Should there be any form of human society that logically precedes or is in any way above the individuals that compose it?

C. If such a society either exists or is desirable, what are its characteristics?

VII. Power (Authority)

A. Should any individual or group of individuals be able to control, determine, or direct the actions of others?

B. If this is desirable, what form or forms should it take? Should it be limited or unlimited? Who limits and how?

VIII. Justice

A. It is usually assumed that justice is desirable, but what is it? Is it individual or social?

B. Who decides the characteristics of justice? Who enforces these characteristics?

IX. The End of Society or Government

A. For what purposes does society or government exist?

B. Who decides these purposes or are they consciously chosen?

X. Structural Characteristics of Government

A. What is the best or best possible form of government? Why?

B. Are there alternative forms of government that are equally valid? What is the standard of judgment? Who decides?

The first of these questions concerns human nature, and thus we ask first, what are the basic characteristics of man as man, and second, what effect, if any, does the nature of man have upon the political system? The first question is answered in surprisingly similar ways by all of the ideologies with the exception of fascism and national socialism. Communism, democracy, and anarchism argue that man is fundamentally capable of a high degree of community spirit and good feeling toward his fellow man. The ideologies of the developing countries do not address themselves to this question specifically, and fascism and national socialism stress the factors of hate and fear rather than the good in man. There is also underlying much of communism, democracy, and anarchism a belief that man is fundamentally rational. Nationalism, fascism, and national socialism, and, owing to the influence of nationalism, the ideologies of developing countries, do not stress man's rationality to the extent that the other ideologies do. Fascism and national socialism clearly stress man's irrational side. The New Left attempts to recognize both sides. Nationalism, and again because of the influence of nationalism, the ideologies of the developing nations stress the emotional, not specifically the irrational, characteristics of man. The second question, What effect does the nature of man have upon the political system?, is not answered by any of the ideologies. This is probably true because man in the 20th century is not very concerned with human nature. The question is unanswerable, so it is seldom raised. Therefore, contemporary ideologies are not going to address themselves to the question of the effect of the nature of man upon the political system.

The second set of questions, the origin of society and government or the state, are also, on the whole, ignored by these ideologies. We have indicated at places that both traditional Marxism and certain arguments for democracy do talk about these origins, but again contemporary political ideologies are not very often concerned with such questions. Ideologies today are not concerned with these questions for the simple reason that many people view them as irrelevant. Man everywhere finds himself in society and ruled by government, and therefore the question of how this happened does not seem to be very important.

Anarchism, because it rejects the notion of government and the state, does deal to some extent with their origins. Generally, the conclusion is that man at some time or other formed a society for protection. Some anarchists argue that government was also formed out of society for protection or security. Others argue that government came about simply by usurpation on the part of some group within society. The reasoning behind both arguments is that each tends to accept society as a necessary form of cooperation, whereas government is rejected as not necessary. It can and should be done away with because it stifles man's ability to cooperate with his fellow man.

Questions in the third set, centering on political obligations, are answered by all of the ideologies, but in some, such as democracy, the answers are so diverse and so varied that it is difficult even to summarize them. Why does or should man obey the government or, in order to include anarchism, should he at all? The simplest answer is of course given by anarchism: There is no reason why man should obey government. The ideologies of the developing nations also give fairly direct and simple answers. First, man should obey government because of the economic benefits it will be able to give him. Second, he should obey for security. Third, and this would include nationalism, man should obey government because government is the symbol of the unity of the nation.

Fascism and national socialism answer the question along the lines of the third answer of the ideologies of the developing nations, but for fascism and national socialism the compulsion to obey must be much stronger than the symbolic representation. Government does provide security and economic benefits, but it must also be obeyed because it is the government— because the system of leadership demands obedience. Man must obey because it is his role to obey and to be led. Communism would argue that the dictatorship of the proletariat should be obeyed because it provides security and economic benefits in the period of transition from bourgeois society to a full Communist society. At the same time, the individual living under the capitalist society has no specific obligation to obey that society. As a matter of fact, the ideology implies that the proletariat has a specific obligation to attempt to overthrow the government. This is not as true in contemporary communism as it was in early Communist doctrine. It would probably be more accurate to say today that a member of the proletariat in a bourgeois or capitalist society neither has a specific obligation to obey or to attempt to overthrow that government.

Democracy is a much more complicated problem because of the wide variety of reasons given for justifying obedience, some of which are similar to the reasons given in other ideologies. These reasons may be summarized somewhat as follows: (1) security, (2) other benefits, (3) requirement by the community justifying obedience itself, and (4) because it is within the power of the citizen to change the entire system while still obeying. Democracy raises other problems with regard to revolution and the possibility of disobedience. Contemporary democratic theory is beginning to accept the idea of disobedience without revolution (this was discussed in the chapter on democracy). Most democratic ideology rejects revolution within a democracy because of reason four for obedience given above. As we saw in the chapter on the New Left, there is a basic disagreement over the question of violence, but there is an acceptance of disobedience and revolution.

The fourth set of questions concerns liberty. Again, nationalism is not directly relevant here. Communism would argue that under Full Communism the individual is given complete liberty. Under the dictatorship of the proletariat, the individual must have sharply curtailed liberty in order to achieve the transition. Fascism and national socialism would essentially consider the question of liberty irrelevant. The individual's freedom, such as it is, is found entirely in giving himself up to the state. The ideologies of the developing nations do not directly address themselves to the question, and it is very difficult to draw any conclusions. Anarchism, since there is no government, has a system of complete liberty. The New Left comes closest to anarchism. Democracy again is the most complicated of the ideologies. Democracy contends that it provides for liberty within the system, but at the same time, liberty must exist in a limited way; the problem for the democratic system is to maintain a system in which the people of the country are willing and able to limit themselves, both individually and through the legal system, so that the liberty of one individual does not, in fact, infringe upon the liberty of another.

The fifth set of questions concerns equality. Clearly fascism and national socialism reject any form of equality. Nationalism and the ideologies of the developing nations are not directly concerned with the question of equality, although most of the ideologies of the developing countries do include some concern with a general level of economic security that is one aspect of equality. Anarchism generally considers that all individuals must be considered to be equal socially and politically. There is considerable debate among anarchists whether or not economic equality is a worthwhile goal. Communism stresses social equality and includes political equality in the ideal of Full Communism. In the period of the dictatorship of the proletariat, social equality would exist, but political equality would not, because of the necessity of strong power at the top. Economic equality is a goal of communism except that it does not argue for complete economic equality. It argues for an overcoming of the extremes of economic in-equality. This last point would hold true equally well for many demo-cratic theories, including both democratic capitalism and democratic so-cialism, the difference between the two being primarily those of means rather than of ends. Democracy stresses political and legal equality and the equality of opportunity. It does not concern itself as much with economic equality as with the other forms of equality. The New Left is different only in its emphasis on social equality.

The sixth set of questions concerns the problem of community. We have stressed that for nationalism and the ideologies of the developing countries, community is a major concern. For the other ideologies, this point is not as significant, although the notion of the nation or the race in fascism and national socialism has elements of the idea of community within it. The other ideologies tend to accept an idea of community as a goal and are concerned with how one achieves it but are not very conclu-sive in their answers. The New Left is fundamentally concerned with the question of a community. It believes that one of the most important things that must be done in contemporary society is to redevelop this sense of community that has disappeared with modern industrialization and specialization.

The question of power is not directly discussed by nationalism or the ideologies of the developing nations. Power for the Communist ideology varies depending on whether you are concerned with the dictatorship of the proletariat or Full Communism. In Full Communism, power would be widely diversified among all individuals. In the dictatorship of the proletariat, power, in fact, rests in the hands of a few at the very top of the Communist party. Some contend that power resides in the party as such, but it would be more accurate to see it in the hands of a few. Fascism and national socialism also invest power in the hands of the very few or one individual at the very top. Democracy argues that power is diversified among all individuals. It would be more accurate to see it in the hands of those actively concerned with the governmental process and actively working within it. There is no focus of power in anarchism; power is centered in each individual separately. In the New Left, power centers in the community.

The next two sets of questions, justice and the end of society or government, may be conveniently collapsed together because each of the ideologies would contend that justice will be found by achieving the end of the ideology or the ends of the society or government. For communism, justice is found in the proletariat owning the means of production and distribution. For the democrat, justice is found in the individual citizen controlling his own destiny through the political system. In even stronger terms, this is true for the New Left. For the Fascist and National Socialist, justice is found in the individual giving himself up willingly and thoroughly to the state. Justice for the ideologies of the developing countries is found in economic, political, and social advancement. For the anarchist, justice is found in the end of government and the achievement of a society based on the individual.

The final set of questions concerns the structural characteristics of government. Clearly, this is irrelevant to nationalism, anarchism, Full Communism, and the New Left. The others do not consistently answer the question in a way that makes valid generalizations possible.

In the answers to these questions, we are able to see the positions of the ideologies toward the fundamental political questions. We note that the answers vary considerably from ideology to ideology but also that the answers are sometimes quite divergent within a given ideology. This overview gives us some basis of comparison of the political aspects of the ideologies. In order to fully understand the value system of the ideology, we must look at certain other social institutions. Therefore, a second stage of comparison of the ideologies must look at these other subsystems of the social system.

The first is the social stratification and mobility system. Again, nationalism and the ideologies of the developing countries are not directly relevant to this system. Communism argues that there will be no social stratification and hence no social mobility system within Full Communism. Under the dictatorship of the proletariat, the only stratification system that should exist would be that between the proletariat and the remnants of the bourgeoisie and the peasantry. The only form of mobility that would be possible would be for the bourgeoisie and the peasantry to move into the proletariat. In fact, the dictatorship of the proletariat has produced a new social stratification system which establishes a class of technocrats who essentially operate the government, the Communist party, and the various important institutions of the country. Therefore, the Communist social stratification system is based in large part upon two factors, first, membership in the Communist party and, second, education.

The democratic social stratification and mobility system is based primarily on money and education. Democratic countries tend to view their stratification systems in purely economic terms, with some questions about certain relatively low-paid professional groups such as college professors and high school teachers. The primary means of mobility in the democratic system is education. As we noticed in the chapter on the New Left, its main concern with the social stratification and mobility system is that each individual must be capable of mobility. There is not any defined system by which mobility can be achieved. The New Left rejects any stratification system as being irrelevant, even though it accepts the idea of there being some differences among individuals within society. For fascism and national socialism, stratification is based on race, indications of loyalty to the nation, service in the party, and service to the state. Mobility is based on the same standards. For anarchism, there would be no social stratification system and hence no mobility system.

The socialization system is made up of various institutions in society that help to give to an individual the values of that society. The primary institutions of socialization are the family, the educational system, the religious system, and, in modern societies, the mass media. The individual child gains ideas about the life around him before he is capable of articulating those ideas himself. He hears his parents give positive or negative connotations to certain words and phrases that the child can identify but for which he has no meaning. For example, a child in the United States might gain a positive connotation with the word *democratic* and a negative connotation with the word *republican* from parents that were strongly in favor of the Democratic party. The child continues throughout life hearing various words given particular connotations.

Again, in the United States as an example, the child might very often hear the word *communism* connected with the idea of evil or something bad. Therefore, before the individual is at all capable of understanding what communism is about, he is convinced that it is bad, and this type of connotation is extremely difficult to change. Therefore, these institutions of socialization are extremely important if a society is going to be able to imbue individuals with the values of the system. Thus, it is instructive to look at some of the attitiudes of these ideologies toward the major institution of socialization.

It is noteworthy, first, that communism, fascism, and national socialism as well as the ideologies of the developing countries, almost without exception, hold that the mass media must be carefully controlled so that it will present a picture of the system to the public that has positive connotations. Anarchism and the New Left tend to argue for a completely unlimited mass media. Democracy comes very close to this, only limiting the media in cases of libel and only in relatively rare cases. Democracies have found a greater problem, though, in connection with the unwillingness of governmental officials to give the mass media complete information, thus, in a sense, controlling the media.

One would think that communism, fascism, national socialism, and the ideologies of the developing countries would also argue for control of the other institutions of socialization, and in some cases they do. Communism clearly argues for a great control of religion because it is seen as a direct threat to the ideology. Fascism and national socialism tended, on the other hand, to view religion as a positive support of the nationalism that was so important to the ideology, and in many cases, the religious system did, in fact, support fascism and national socialism, or at least did not oppose it very actively. The ideologies of the developing countries seem, on the whole, to have avoided the question of religion. Neither anarchism, democracy, nor the New Left is concerned with controlling religion, although in anarchism one often finds an antipathy toward religion. Many anarchists believe that religion consistently supports the state and thus is opposed to the anarchist philosophy. Most, but not all, democratic ideologies and democratic systems argue for a separation between the religious system and the political system, but they also seem to believe that religion can be a positive support for the political system of democracy.

Every ideology is concerned with using the educational system as a direct support for the ideology. All of the ideologies believe that the educational system is the most potent force of socialization within the social system and believe that the educational system must be used to support the values of the society or the ideology. On the other hand, none of the ideologies, with the partial exceptions of anarchism and the New Left, says much about changing the family system in such a way that it might bring about support for the ideology. Attempts have been made in some Communist countries to bring about such changes, but they have so far been unsuccessful. It is probably better policy to attempt to imbue the parents with the values that one wishes to have passed on to the children and if the parents do, in fact, accept the values, they will be automatically passed on to the children. Therefore, it is not really necessary to tamper with the family system.

In each of the ideologies that we have discussed, a considerable amount of time has been spent analyzing the last aspect of the social system, the economic system. It is not necessary here to repeat those arguments. It is only necessary to say that each of the ideologies has differing attitudes toward the economic system. Communism has combined with an authoritarian political system a state socialist economic system. Democracy has combined with its political system either a capitalist form of economic system or a socialist one. Fascism and national socialism have authoritarian political systems combined with slightly modified capitalist systems. The ideologies of the developing countries all talk about socialist economic systems, but we noted the wide difference between the very moderate reform systems that are essentially capitalistic and the state socialist systems at the other extreme. Anarchism, we indicated, was unclear concerning the appropriate economic system for its political, or one might better say, its apolitical system. The New Left accepts democratic socialism.

These comments have been very general, but hopefully they provide some basis for comparison among the ideologies. It is important for a student of contemporary political ideologies to understand both the similarities and the differences among these ideologies. We do not know what the future holds in store for any of these, but it is important for us to understand what each of these ideologies accepts so that we will be able to evaluate them objectively.

INDEX

*This book has been set in 11 point Fairfield,
leaded 3 points, and 10 point Fairfield, leaded 2
points. Chapter numbers and Chapter titles are
in 30 point and 18 point Corvinus Medium.
The size of the type page is 27 by 44½ picas.*